P9-DWE-060

CULTURES OF THE WORLD®

EL SALVADOR

Erin Foley/Rafiz Hapipi

MARSHALL CAVENDISH BENCHMARK

NEW YORK

PICTURE CREDITS
Cover photo: © Corbis: Linda Richardson
AFP: 93, 129 • Camera Press: 36, 37, 39, 62, 119, 122 • Corbis Inc.: 25 • Douglas Donne Bryant
Stock Photography: 19, 27, 41, 67, 69, 70, 74, 76, 96, 97, 105, 110 • Erin Foley: 86 • The Image
Bank: 17, 43, 107 • Björn Klingwall: 60 (top), 66, 124 (bottom) • Life File Photo Library: 3, 4, 7,
10, 11, 12, 13, 16, 21, 22, 24, 33, 34, 38, 46, 58, 65, 68, 72, 73, 79 (bottom), 82, 84, 91, 95, 100, 101,
102 (both), 112, 113 (bottom), 116, 121, 124 (top), 126, 127 • Lonely Planet Images: 1, 6, 9, 18, 30,
48, 53, 54, 55, 56, 64, 80, 98, 106, 120 • Reuters: 47, 114 • Reuters/Juan Carlos Ulate: 49 • Reuters/
Luis Galdamez: 5, 40, 51, 90 • David Simson: 8, 14, 15, 28, 31, 32, 42, 44, 57, 59, 60 (bottom), 61,
77, 78, 79 (top), 81, 83, 87, 88, 89, 99, 103, 104, 108, 109, 113 (top and center), 123, 125, 128, 130
• Times Editions: 131

PRECEDING PAGE
Young Salvadoran children dressed for a procession in honor of the Virgin of Guadalupe.

Marshall Cavendish Benchmark
99 White Plains Road
Tarrytown, NY 10591
Website: www.marshallcavendish.us

© Times Editions Private Limited 1995
© Marshall Cavendish International (Asia) Private Limited 2005
All rights reserved. First edition 1995. Second edition 2005.

® "Cultures of the World" is a registered trademark of Marshall Cavendish Corporation.

Originated and designed by Times Editions
An imprint of Marshall Cavendish International (Asia) Private Limited
A member of Times Publishing Limited

Library of Congress Cataloging-in-Publication Data
Foley, Erin, 1967-
   El Salvador / by Erin Foley. – 2nd ed.
     p. cm. – (Cultures of the world)
   Summary: "Explores the geography, history, government, economy, people,
     and culture of El Salvador" – Provided by publisher.
   Includes bibliographical references and index.
   ISBN 0-7614-1967-5
   1. El Salvador – Juvenile literature. I. Title: Salvador. II. Title. III. Series.
   F1483.2.F65 2005
   972.84 — dc22   2005009360

Printed in China

7 6 5 4 3 2 1

CONTENTS

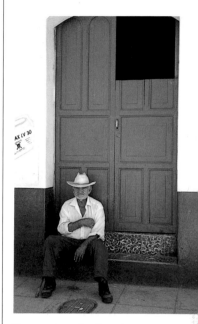

The vast majority of Salvadorans are of mixed Indian and Spanish descent. It is quite common to see the men wearing Western clothing and straw cowboy hats.

3

Salvadoran firefighters and ambulance workers are easily spotted in their bright uniforms.

INTRODUCTION

DESPITE BEING BLESSED with a landscape of great beauty and fertility, and a people who have shown immense courage and spirit in the face of centuries of poverty and repression, El Salvador is a country that has experienced social, economic, and political problems of crisis proportions. Since colonial times, overpopulation and the scarcity of land have caused bitter fighting among its people and have affected every aspect of its development. A civil war that tore the country apart for 12 years and left some 75,000 people dead finally came to an end in 1992, and the process of rebuilding the country is under way.

This book in the series *Cultures of the World* explores some of the factors that have contributed to El Salvador's turbulent past and takes a look at the lifestyle and culture of the people who call this lush but harsh country home.

GEOGRAPHY

EL SALVADOR is a beautiful tropical land of ruined temples and ancient Mayan cities, volcanoes, mountain lakes, and Pacific black-sand beaches. Bordered by Guatemala to the west, Honduras to the north and east, and the Pacific Ocean to the south, the landscape is dominated by two parallel east-west mountain ranges that divide the country into its three main regions: the northern mountains and plain, the central region, and the southern coastal lowlands. El Salvador is only slightly larger than the state of Massachusetts and is the smallest country in Central America. With more than 811 people per square mile, however, it is more densely populated than any other mainland country in the Western Hemisphere.

Left: **A sweeping view of the Planes Renderos. A landscape of mountains and fertile plains is characteristic of the central region.**

Opposite: **A view of a residential area in Cuscatlán.**

The fertile lowland plains run in a narrow strip between the central highland region and the Pacific Ocean.

TOPOGRAPHY

It is hard to go anywhere in El Salvador without seeing a volcano. Scattered along the central region and interspersed with large, open plateaus is a chain of 20 volcanoes. These volcanoes, several of which are still active, have played a fundamental role in the country's history and development.

It is no accident that there is a major town at the base of each of the highest volcanoes—Santa Ana, San Vicente, San Miguel, and San Salvador— all towering 6,000 to 8,000 feet (1,830 to 2,438 m) above sea level. The volcanoes feed the land below with a mixture of ash, lava, and sediment that has made the soil extremely fertile and able to support large concentrations of people for thousands of years. Though the central region makes up only a quarter of El Salvador's land, the region contains the country's biggest cities and most of the population.

The central highlands slope down to the south to a narrow strip of land along the Pacific coast. The lowland soil is enriched by runoff from numerous small rivers that drain from the central highlands. High temperatures year-round, in addition to heavy rains, ensure that the land is thick with foliage and good for agriculture.

North of the central region is a broad plain and a band of mountains, where agricultural conditions are less ideal. Lying only 1,300 to 2,000 feet (396 to 610 m) above sea level, the plain suffers from poor drainage and acidic soil, while the steep slopes of the Sierra Madre Mountains running along the border with Honduras suffer from excessive clearing of forests and many years of overfarming.

A LAND OF EARTHQUAKES AND VOLCANOES

El Salvador lies in a precarious position, directly at the meeting place of three tectonic plates that cause frequent earthquakes and volcanic eruptions as they rub against each other. Although the movement of each of these tectonic plates is a barely perceptible 6 inches (15 cm) per year or less, over long periods of time it is enough to create chains of volcanic ridges and earthquake fault lines.

A view of the Cerro Verde, Izalco, and Santa Ana volcanic mountains in Santa Ana Province.

Earthquakes completely destroyed El Salvador's capital city twice, in 1756 and 1854, and badly damaged it several times in the last century. In 1986, in the midst of the civil war, an earthquake killed over a thousand people. Between January and February 2001 a series of earthquakes and thousands of aftershocks hit El Salvador. On January 13 an earthquake that measured 7.6 on the Richter scale took more than a thousand lives, while exactly a month later another earthquake killed about 400 people. Many more were injured or left homeless. While the 2001 earthquakes were still fresh on peoples' minds, there was another on December 13, 2004. Thousands of Salvadorans left their homes in panic. Fortunately there were no reported casualties, and only the telephone lines were affected.

This building was one of many destroyed by the 1986 earthquake.

THE IZALCO VOLCANO

The Izalco volcano is located in the western region of El Salvador. Its earliest recorded eruption was in 1700. Since then, it has erupted regularly and is nicknamed the Lighthouse of the Pacific: At night the molten lava running down its sides turns the volcano into a brightly glowing beacon that can be seen from miles out to sea. Now black and bare, Izalco is still classified as an active volcano, but it has not erupted since 1966. The volcano stands at a height of about 6,004 feet (1,830 m).

Volcanoes, too, have brought destruction to many Salvadoran towns. The twin-peaked San Salvador volcano, which towers above the country's capital, has not erupted since 1917. However, the town of San Miguel has suffered 10 eruptions in the last century from its namesake volcano. Despite their destructive nature, volcanoes have been a blessing for El Salvador, making the soil extremely fertile and providing an alternative energy source in the form of geothermal energy.

RIVERS AND LAKES

El Salvador has over 300 rivers, and the Lempa River is the largest. It enters El Salvador in the northwest and runs for 145 miles (235 km) across the country before flowing into the Pacific Ocean. The Lempa was once a major navigation and transportation route, but its importance now lies in its hydroelectric dams, the Cerrón Grande and the Cinco de Noviembre. The power harnessed by these dams helps El Salvador reduce its dependence on imported petroleum. The two dams have created lakes, adding to the natural and volcanic lakes the country already has.

Many of the volcanic craters in the central region have flooded to form beautiful lakes bordered by steep, green slopes. The largest of these is Lake Ilopango, which is located just east of San Salvador, and Lake Coatepeque in the west. Both are popular recreation spots for Salvadorans.

Lake Coatepeque, a clean, sparkling blue crater lake on the eastern slopes of the Santa Ana volcano, is a popular spot for swimming, boating, and fishing.

CLIMATE

Lying close to the equator, El Salvador experiences little variation in temperature throughout the year, and seasons are marked more by the difference in levels of rainfall. Temperatures do, however, vary between the three main regions, due to differences in altitude.

The rainy season, known as *invierno* (in-vee-AIR-noh), or winter, lasts from May through October. During these months, it usually rains every evening, often in a downpour. June is the wettest month. The average total annual rainfall during *invierno* is about 80 inches (203 cm).

The dry season, known as *verano* (vay-RAH-noh), or summer, is from November through April, during which time much of El Salvador is dry and dusty. The hottest months are March and April.

The moderate climate of the central region is typified by San Salvador: at 2,156 feet (657 m) above sea level, the capital's temperature ranges from 60°F to 94°F (16°C to 34°C). The coastal lowlands are usually much hotter, with an average of 83°F (28°C) and high humidity. Northern mountain areas average only 64°F (18°C), and temperatures occasionally drop to near freezing.

The cool, clear springs at Los Chorros, a park near San Salvador, provide a welcome break from El Salvador's tropical heat.

FLORA AND FAUNA

Palm trees and tropical fruit trees, such as coconut, mango, and tamarind, flourish in the hot, humid coastal plains, as do armadillos, iguanas, and snakes. El Salvador's birdlife includes wild ducks, white and royal herons, blue jays, and the urraca—a grey-headed, blue-breasted bird noted for its call, which resembles a scoffing laugh. Turtles, reptiles, and a wide variety of fish populate El Salvador's many rivers, lakes, and coastal waters.

Large-scale deforestation and agriculture have destroyed much of El Salvador's animal and plant life, both of which are not as rich as those found in other Central American countries. Rich stands of ebony, cedar, and mahogany once covered much of the country, but the trees were cleared to open up land for cultivation and to provide valuable wood

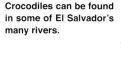

Crocodiles can be found in some of El Salvador's many rivers.

for export. The mountainous regions are mostly grassland with some remnants of oak and pine forests. Formerly abundant species of cats and monkeys have disappeared from the mountains. Deer, pumas, coyotes, tapirs, and peccaries (wild pigs) can still be found there, however, the destruction of much of their habitat has decreased their numbers.

MONTE CRISTO CLOUD FOREST

At the 7,931-foot (2,417-m) summit of Monte Cristo Mountain, near where the borders of El Salvador, Guatemala, and Honduras meet, lies El Trifinio, an international nature reserve protected by all three countries. Inside El Trifinio is the Monte Cristo cloud forest, the last vestige of rain forest in El Salvador and one of the few remaining cloud forests in Central America. A cloud forest is a tropical forest located at a high altitude and usually covered by clouds.

Colorful flowers such as these can still be found in parts of El Salvador despite large-scale deforestation.

At Monte Cristo the oak and laurel trees grow almost 100 feet (31 m) tall, and their branches and leaves intertwine to form a canopy that is impenetrable to sunlight. With 100 percent humidity and 80 inches (203 cm) of rain a year, the forest is constantly dripping wet, creating an ideal habitat for a wide variety of exotic plants, including mushrooms, orchids, lichens, mosses, and ferns.

The cloud forest's protected microclimates also support an abundance of animal life not found elsewhere in El Salvador: spider monkeys, two-fingered anteaters, porcupines, spotted and hooded skunks, red and grey squirrels, and opossums. Monte Cristo is home to woodpeckers, nightingales, hummingbirds, white-faced quails, striped owls, and green toucans.

The pyramid at Tazumal is thought to have been built in A.D. 980, at the height of the Mayan civilization in Central America. The pyramid has now been restored.

MAYAN RUINS

Archaeologists have unearthed remains of ancient cities at Tazumal and San Andrés proving that the Maya, one of the world's great civilizations, inhabited this region in 5000 B.C.

Tazumal, which in the Mayan language Quiché, means pyramid where the victims were burned, has a stepped pyramid as well as the remains of a large courtyard used for ritual ball games of the Maya. The clay vessels, ritual ornaments, and sculptures found at the ruins demonstrate that the Maya engaged in trade with people from as far away as Panama and Mexico. Efforts to uncover the wonders of the Mayan civilization started in the late 19th century. However, Tazumal has only been partially excavated because much of the 10-square-mile (6,400-square-acre) site is buried under the present-day town of Chalchuapa.

San Andrés, just west of San Salvador, was inhabited by a succession of Maya, Aztec, and Pipil Indians. Pottery, grinding stones, and flint have been found, and a courtyard has been excavated.

In 1978 archaeologists discovered another ancient city at Joya de Cerén. The site was buried under 20 feet (6 m) of volcanic ash, which preserved artifacts providing clues to the inhabitants' daily lives. For this, it has been nicknamed the Pompeii of Central America.

CITIES

For thousands of years, most of the people of El Salvador have chosen to live in the central plains, where the soil is rich and fertile. Spanish colonial settlements, many of them built on the sites of ancient Indian cities, have now become the principal cities of San Salvador, Santa Ana, and San Miguel.

San Salvador, the capital, now bustles with 1.8 million people—almost a third of the country's total population—in the city center and suburbs. Following a pattern that has been repeated in cities the world over, San Salvador has been a magnet for Salvadorans fleeing poverty and warfare in rural areas, but has failed to meet the increased demand for housing and jobs. The city reflects the huge gap between rich and poor in El Salvador: established, luxurious neighborhoods overlook the city from the surrounding hilltops, while shantytowns of makeshift huts made out of cardboard, tin, or mud cram the outskirts.

Santa Ana, with a population of half a million, is the transportation hub and urban center for the western half of the country. Its Indian name, Cihuatehuacán, means place of holy women.

San Miguel, a lively market town of about 245,000, attracts visitors from all over the eastern half of the country.

The contrast of concrete buildings alongside makeshift cardboard and tin structures show the disparity between the rich and poor dwellers in the cities.

HISTORY

THE HISTORY OF EL SALVADOR stretches back thousands of years to a time when Indians inhabited the region, living off the fertile soil and honing their knowledge of astronomy and mathematics. The Spanish Conquest in 1528 began a turbulent era that continues today. Claiming the land for themselves, the Spanish pushed the Indians into servitude and poverty and established the power of the oligarchy and the Roman Catholic Church. Even after independence, the landowning elite, the Catholic Church, and the military worked hand in hand to protect their power and wealth. Despite often brutal repression at the hands of the military, the peasants continued to fight against their landlessness and poverty. In 1980 rebellion escalated into civil war. Only since peace was negotiated in 1992, bringing promises of major economic and social reform, has El Salvador been able to look forward to a brighter future.

Left: **Rebel leaders Joaquín Villalobos and Jorge Shafik Hándel at a press conference at the end of the civil war in 1992 that saw the death of about 75,000 Salvadorans.**

Opposite: **Pottery, grinding stones, and sculptures such as this one have been excavated in the Mayan ruins in San Andrés, just west of the capital, San Salvador.**

ANCIENT CIVILIZATIONS

By the time the Spanish arrived in Central America in the 16th century, the Indians had made agricultural advances far beyond those of Europe.

The true discoverers of the Americas were a group of Asian peoples who entered North America after crossing the Bering Strait, which separates the Asian and North American continents at their closest point. This started around 20,000 to 35,000 years ago, and they slowly migrated southward into Central and South America.

The Olmecs, who arrived in about 2000 B.C., were the first ancient civilization to leave their mark in Central America. Although much about their culture remains a mystery, they are known to have made technical, artistic, and scientific advances that laid the groundwork for the extraordinary cultural achievements of the Maya.

The Maya settled in villages in about 1500 B.C. Guatemala was the center of their civilization, but they also lived in the western half of El Salvador. The Maya built their economy around agriculture, cultivating an enormous variety of plants. In addition to corn, they raised several types of beans, gourds, squash, and other produce unknown in Europe at the time, such as pineapples, tomatoes, peanuts, green peppers, cacao, vanilla, avocados, and chili peppers.

As they developed more and more advanced systems of producing food, the Maya were able to devote more time and energy to developing their skills in the arts and sciences. In hieroglyphic writing, astronomy, and mathematics, the Mayan Indians were far ahead of any other people in the New World.

The Mayan civilization declined after A.D. 900. It was at this time that the Toltec Empire reached its peak of power and prosperity. The Nahuatl-speaking Toltecs disappeared around the 12th century, opening the way for the Chichimec peoples. The Aztecs were among the Chichimec peoples to move in from the north to occupy the region.

The Pipil, a Nahua people closely related to the Aztecs, are thought to have migrated south from Mexico. Around the 11th century the Pipil nation covered parts of what is now El Salvador and Guatemala. They called their new land Cuscatlán, or Land of the Jewel.

By the time of the Spanish Conquest in the 16th century, there was a large class of artisans and specialists, including carpenters, potters, stonemasons, hunters, dancers, and musicians, who enjoyed a position of high honor and responsibility. Society was highly organized, with a strict hierarchy (priests, warriors, and bureaucrats occupied the top rungs of the ladder) and a well-developed government and judicial system. Books made from bark were used to record calendars, astronomical tables, taxes, dynastic history, and court records. Religion was the major focus of Nahua culture, and priests played a key role in the daily life of the people.

The Olmec Boulder in Chalchuapa is evidence of Olmec presence in what is now El Salvador. Monumental stone carvings and sculptures were important elements of Olmec culture.

A statue of Christopher Columbus outside the National Palace is a symbol of the Spanish conquest of Central America.

THE SPANISH CONQUEST

Hungry for gold and silver, the Spanish conquistador Pedro de Alvarado first attacked Cuscatlán in June 1524. The Pipil Indians proved to be formidable opponents, however, and Alvarado's men were forced to withdraw to Guatemala. The Spaniards later returned and finally succeeded in defeating the Pipil in 1528. They renamed the small colony El Salvador, or The Savior, but were disappointed to find little gold or silver there.

The Spanish settlers who followed realized that El Salvador's wealth lay in the richness of its soil and the size of its Indian population. Knowing that huge profits could be reaped by cultivating single crops for export, the Spanish Crown took the land away from the Indians and parceled it out to a handful of settlers. These settlers were popularly known as the 14 Families, although the actual number was higher. They created enormous plantations to grow crops, such as cacao (for chocolate), indigo (a natural dye) and, later, coffee. They then looked to the Indians for labor.

The Indians, deprived of their livelihood, found themselves forced to work on the plantations under slave-like conditions, serve in the Spanish army, and pay monetary tributes to the local authorities. Many Indians rose up in protest, but their machetes were no match for the Spaniards' guns.

INDEPENDENCE

The colonists in Central America declared their independence from Spain on September 15, 1821. Two years later, they attempted to create a confederation of states—similar to the United States of America—by forming a union called the United Provinces of Central America, but ideological differences between the state governments caused the confederation to fall apart. El Salvador finally declared its independence as a sovereign country in January 1841.

Independence failed to bring about any improvement to the everyday lives of most Salvadorans. The government eliminated the last communal Indian farms and introduced antivagrancy laws that prevented Indians from looking for new land and forced them to work for the large landowners. The country's power and wealth remained concentrated in the hands of the landowning 14 Families. Strongly supported by the Catholic Church, this closely knit group exercised their control through the government and a newly created National Guard, and thus managed to preserve their position and suppress any dissent.

In the 20th century the 14 Families controlled about 60 percent of El Salvador's land and more than half of its wealth.

THE AQUINO UPRISING

In 1833 Anastasio Aquino, an Indian whose brother had been imprisoned by a wealthy planter, led the most famous of many revolts against the Spanish colonists. He rallied Indian and mestizo peasants to protest against the government and the forced conscription of farm workers.

The strength and unity of the month-long uprising posed a serious threat to the government, but the Indians were soon defeated by the heavy cannons of the government forces. Aquino was captured and executed, but he is remembered as a national hero today.

LA MATANZA

La Matanza, or The Slaughter, of 1932 is one of the great tragedies in El Salvador's history and was an early sign of the lengths to which the oligarchy was prepared to go in order to preserve their wealth and power.

The year 1931 was a time of economic hardship. The Great Depression abroad caused a sharp drop in prices for coffee, El Salvador's main export crop, and the plight of the already poor Indian peasants became even worse when wages and employment levels tumbled further. The creation of a Salvadoran Communist party by university student Augustín Farabundo Martí made the establishment nervous. In December 1931 the military deposed President Arturo Araújo, who was elected to his post the year before but faced rejection by the elite because of the social reforms he proposed. The military installed his vice-president, General Maximiliano Hernández Martínez, in his place.

Farabundo started agitating for change, and in January 1932 Indian insurgents in several rural areas rose against the system of land ownership that had impoverished them. Military forces quickly suppressed the rebel forces and executed Farabundo. Intent on deterring any further protests, government soldiers systematically killed thousands of peasants and Indians who had not even participated in the uprising. Estimates of the number who died range from 15,000 to 30,000.

Rebel leader Augustín Farabundo Martí's name lives on in the guerrilla group Frente Farabundo Martí de Liberación Nacional (FMLN), whose main aim is a fairer distribution of wealth.

REBELLION AND REPRESSION

La Matanza failed in preventing the continued and mounting pressure for political and economic reforms. In the 1960s representatives from the government, the opposition, and labor and business groups recommended the large-scale redistribution of land to the farmers. Conservative members of the government, the military, and the landowning elite, however, refused to have anything to do with reform. The conservative forces reasserted their power by rigging the presidential election in 1972. When it appeared that the victor was José Napoleón Duarte, the moderate, reformist candidate from the Christian Democratic Party, he was arrested and exiled.

Mourners carry the coffins of demonstrators, who were shot dead by the police.

Social unrest and political violence began to increase. Guerrilla groups grew larger and bolder, and mass demonstrations and strikes became more frequent, all of which prompted increasingly brutal suppression by the military against anyone who was even suspected of being a subversive.

The United States wanted to support the battle against popular movements in Central America, which the United States saw as Marxist-based. Honduras was a center for this battle.

Death squads, funded by the oligarchy and organized by the military, kidnapped, tortured, and killed thousands of civilians that supported or were thought to support reform. The victims were snatched away suddenly and usually never seen alive again. They came to be known as Los Desaparecidos, or The Disappeared, as knowledge of their abduction, whereabouts, and fate was denied by the authorities.

THE EL MOZOTE MASSACRE

In early December 1981 the Salvadoran army's U.S.-trained Atlacatl Battalion, led by Lieutenant Colonel Domingo Monterrosa Barrios, carried out one of the largest massacres in modern Latin American history. In the mountain villages of El Mozote, Los Toriles, La Joya, Jocote Amarillo, Rancheria, and Cerro Pando, Monterrosa and his men killed an estimated 1,000 people. The massacre was named after the largest village in which it took place.

The killings were part of an army operation, called Operation Rescue, to break the guerrilla strongholds in the northern mountain region of Morazán. Although El Mozote itself was not reputed to be a guerrilla town, it was in the heart of what the army referred to as the Red Zones. Soldiers carried out a sweep of the entire area. In some villages they executed only people they believed to be guerrilla sympathizers, but in El Mozote and surrounding hamlets they killed everyone. The bodies were left as they were and the buildings set on fire.

Although eyewitness reports soon reached the outside world, Salvadoran and U.S. officials denied that a massacre had taken place. The U.S. Congress was in the middle of debating whether to cut off aid to El Salvador. The U.S. government could not send aid to countries whose governments violated human rights, so the Reagan administration claimed that the Salvadoran government was making progress on human rights in order to be able to continue its policy of fighting Communism in El Salvador.

It was not until after the peace accord was signed 11 years later that the truth was finally established. A team from the world-renowned Argentine Forensic Anthropology Unit (EAAF) began digging in El Mozote and found hundreds of skulls, bones, and U.S. weapons and ammunition. The U.N.-appointed Truth Commission concluded that a massacre of over a thousand civilians had indeed occurred, and that the Atlacatl Battalion was responsible. In light of the findings, the Clinton administration publicly changed the U.S. government's stand that the massacre did not happen. Exhumations by the EAAF resumed in 1999 to further document what actually happened and to allow relatives of the dead to conduct a proper burial for the victims.

CIVIL WAR

Late 1979 and early 1980 was a crucial time in El Salvador's history. Reformist young officers deposed President Carlos Humberto Romero. They set up a coalition junta that pledged sweeping land reforms and an end to repression. José Napoleón Duarte returned from exile, and hopes for a new and improved El Salvador ran high. Inevitably, however, the junta faced strong opposition from both the guerrillas and the rightwing factions of the army, and death squad activity increased.

Catholic priests and nuns began to speak out against the repression and poverty, and they too became government targets. Archbishop Oscar Arnulfo Romero was assassinated on March 24, 1980, while saying Mass. Later that year, four churchwomen from the United States were raped and killed by the military as they were driving through the countryside.

Full-scale civil war between the rebels and government forces erupted. The United States believed the rebels were supported by communist nations and feared the spread of Communism in Central America, so it supplied economic and military aid to El Salvador. José Napoleón Duarte was elected president in 1984, but his inability to bring an end to the fighting, coupled with corruption within his party, caused his downfall. The turmoil and destruction caused by the ongoing war affected every aspect of life in El Salvador, and by the late 1980s, the country's social, economic, and political problems had reached crisis proportions.

Paramedics attend to a wounded soldier.

THE ROLE OF THE UNITED STATES

U.S. policy in El Salvador sought to prevent a leftist or communist takeover and to try to support a moderate alternative to military rule by the junta. The United States had supplied large amounts of military and economic aid to help the Salvadoran government fight the rebel forces and support agrarian reform. Although

it stopped short of sending U.S. combat troops, the United States played a significant role in training Salvadoran army battalions, and it supplied the latest in weaponry.

Although Democratic president Jimmy Carter threatened to cut off aid in response to human rights abuses in El Salvador, he was not prepared to take the blame for any advance of Communism that a rebel victory might bring, and so concentrated instead on using military aid and social programs to encourage democracy in El Salvador. His attempts to break the oligarchy and redistribute wealth, however, only strengthened the repressive Salvadoran armed forces.

When Ronald Reagan came to power, the Republican administration called for a strengthening of the U.S. stand against Communism in El Salvador. Around the time that initial reports of the El Mozote massacre were making front-page news in the United States, aid to El Salvador was increased. The Republicans argued that the tolerance of human rights atrocities was deplorable but necessary, because they believed a Communist victory was by far the worst disaster that could befall human rights in Central America. Preserving the Salvadoran government and helping it win the war were of paramount importance.

The Reagan policy on El Salvador failed, and the Bush administration changed it when it came into office by supporting UN efforts for peace negotiations in El Salvador. Later the Clinton administration followed in the same vein by reducing aid to El Salvador and insisting that the Salvadoran government observe the 1992 peace accord terms.

The proliferation of anti-U.S. graffiti is evidence that many Salvadorans saw the role of the United States as interventionist and resented it. "Be a patriot, kill a Yankee" and "Imperialists, get out of El Salvador" are typical slogans *(above)*.

PEACE

In the late 1980s, international pressure to end the war increased. Negotiations between the government and the FMLN guerrillas began in September 1989 but were disrupted by further violence. The FMLN attempted a final offensive to overthrow the Salvadoran government, but failed to rouse enough popular support. The army, for their part, broke into the University of Central America in San Salvador and murdered six Jesuit priests, their housekeeper, and her daughter. These killings shocked international observers as well as people in El Salvador. U.S. aid was halted, and both the goverment and the FMLN invited the United Nations (UN) to mediate. After two years of hard negotiating, a peace agreement was finally signed in January 1992. Under the terms of the agreement, the FMLN became a legal political party. It agreed to lay down its arms in return for wide-ranging reforms, including land redistribution, a substantial decrease in the size and role of the armed forces, and a purge of the worst human rights offenders from the army officer corps. However, the FMLN was discovered to have a number of arms caches belonging to them in the region, and its disarmament was completed only in August 1993. The government, for its part, passed a presidential bill in March 1993 that granted amnesty to people who were guilty of violating human rights before January 1992. Requests were made to review this law, but until 1998 the Supreme Court turned these down. It was only in October 2000 that the Supreme Court changed its position and stated that "judicial officials should make the decision whether or not to prosecute" parties who violated human rights between 1989 and 1994.

By 2004 FMLN had replaced ARENA as the largest single political party in parliament. If the absence of armed combat is taken as a benchmark of peace, then Salvadorans have demonstrated their willingness to sustain it.

The signing of the peace accord on January 16, 1992, at Chapultepec Castle in Mexico marked the end of the most violent period in El Salvador's history.

GOVERNMENT

The armed forces long dominated political life in El Salvador, despite a constitution that describes the country as a democratic republic with an elected president. The oligarchy and the military regularly set democracy aside, using coups, rigged elections, and repression to maintain their power and prestige. Government repression was particularly brutal during the 12-year civil war that ended in 1992. During this period, tens of thousands of ordinary Salvadorans were harassed, tortured, or killed by government forces for speaking out in favor of reform. Killings by paramilitary death squads went not only unpunished but unacknowledged by the courts. The 1992 peace agreement established a framework for reforming the judicial system, electoral process, armed forces, and police. Many of these changes have been highly controversial and difficult to implement, but a degree of progress has been made in some areas despite long delays.

Left: **Children campaign for the ARENA party's candidate. Excitement surrounded the 1994 national elections, the first "open" elections in El Salvador's history.**

Opposite: **The National Palace bears a neoclassical architecture.**

NATIONAL GOVERNMENT

The government is divided into three branches: the executive, the legislative assembly, and the judiciary.

THE EXECUTIVE BRANCH This branch, consisting of the president, the council of ministers, and the undersecretaries of state, is responsible for preparing the budget, managing the armed forces and the security forces, and directing foreign relations. Presidential elections are held every five

The National Palace in San Salvador is the administrative center of the executive branch of government. The building had to be restored after it was seriously damaged in the 1986 earthquake.

years, and presidents cannot serve more than one term of office in a row. Every presidential candidate must belong to a legally recognized political party and needs an absolute majority of the votes in order to win.

THE LEGISLATIVE ASSEMBLY The 84 members of the unicameral Legislative Assembly are also popularly elected, serving renewable three-year terms. The Legislative Assembly controls taxes, sanctions the budget, and ratifies or rejects international treaties.

THE JUDICIARY The most important judicial institution is the Supreme Court of Justice. Composed of the constitutional, civil, and criminal chambers, the Supreme Court rules on the constitutionality of laws and acts as the last level of appeal in civil and criminal cases.

Anti-government graffiti in the Plaza Libertad, San Salvador, reads "Cristiani, President of the Death Squads."

LOCAL GOVERNMENT

El Salvador is divided into 14 administrative departments (equivalent to states in the United States), which in turn are divided into 261 municipalities (equivalent to counties). Each department has a governor and a substitute governor who are appointed by the government.

The citizens of each municipality directly elect their own municipal council, composed of a mayor, a legal representative, and two or more council members, depending on the population of the municipality.

MILITARY RULE

From independence until the peace agreement in 1992, politics in El Salvador had been dominated by the armed forces and the civilian oligarchy. The military protected the wealth and privileges of the oligarchy, while boosting their own status and power. Even in the 1980s, when the military ceded direct rule to civilian governments, they continued to play an influential role in the running of the country.

The officer corps developed its own criteria for advancement and rewards that had more to do with politics than military ability. Those who graduated together from the Gerardo Barrios Military Academy would be promoted together, acquiring wealth and power along the way, and defending each other vigorously against external criticism.

Since the 1992 peace accord, the hold of the military finally broke, as 102 army officers who were named the worst abusers of human rights during the civil war either resigned or were removed from office. Although former president Alfredo Cristiani attracted criticism for failing to replace General Ponce, the former minister of defense, with a civilian, the appointment of Colonel Humberto Corado Figueroa marked a clear end to the influence of the Tandona, the 1966 graduating class that ran the armed forces during much of the civil war.

REFORMS AND GOVERNANCE

The military rule governing El Salvador for half a century was seen as one of the root causes of the country's internal conflicts. Consequently, the peace accord, among other things, sought to restructure and reduce the political influence and autonomy of the armed forces. The negotiations focused on not only putting an end to the conflict, but also putting into motion three transitions simultaneously: from war to peace, from militarization to demilitarization, and from authoritarianism to democracy.

However, the peace accord has been most effective in reforming the armed forces, which no longer plays a part in public security. Other aspects of the agreement, such as allowing Salvadorans to participate in the formulation of social and economic policies, have been ignored.

The judiciary suffers from corruption and inefficiency and is staffed by unqualified personnel. Officers of the National Civilian Police (PNC) are still involved in human rights violations and other criminal activities. In June 2000 the Legislative Assembly authorized reforms to the PNC proposed by a commission that investigated police officers' misconduct. However, the new system has attracted criticism for lacking accountability. It also concentrates power in the hands of the president and the PNC director, clearly undermining the objectives of the peace accord.

In 2002 Amnesty International conducted independent reviews to measure the success of the peace accord. According to its report, human rights violations, a central issue of the agreement, still exist because the people responsible for massacres, assassinations, and death squad atrocities have not been punished yet. The Office of the Human Rights Procurator, which is supposed to uphold human rights in El Salvador, does not receive much support from the government. The office remained without a procurator between 1998 and 2001.

The 1992 reforms outlined in the peace accord include creating a civilian-controlled police force, setting up an intelligence service independent of the armed forces and directly accountable to the president, and reducing the number of armed forces personnel.

THE TRUTH COMMISSION REPORT

The 1992 peace agreement called for a UN-appointed Truth Commission to investigate the most serious human rights violations of the war period and publicize its conclusions. In March 1993 the commission released its report, entitled *From Madness to Hope: the 12-Year Civil War in El Salvador*, containing the results of their investigations.

They found that Roberto d'Aubuisson, former leader of the ARENA party, ordered the killing of Archbishop Oscar Arnulfo Romero *(above)* in 1980; that General René Emilio Ponce, then minister of defense, ordered the killings of six Jesuit priests in 1989; and that the Atlacatl Battalion was responsible for the massacre of 1,000 civilians at El Mozote. The report also revealed abuses carried out by the FMLN during the war, and accused the United States of ignoring Salvadoran human rights abuses in its determination to prevent an FMLN victory.

Although the FMLN, Church, and human rights groups welcomed the report, the Salvadoran government reacted negatively to it, denying many of the accusations. A few days after the release of the report, the Salvadoran government issued amnesty for all those involved in the perpetration of atrocities.

POLITICAL PARTIES

Eleven parties contested the 2003 and 2004 elections in El Salvador. The main political parties in the country are:

Nationalist Republican Alliance (ARENA): Led by Archie Baldocchi Duenas, this ruling rightwing party was founded in 1981. In the 2003 elections, ARENA was defeated by FMLN for the first time and managed to retain ruling powers only after forging a coalition with smaller parties.

FMLN (Farabundo Martí Front for National Liberation): The former guerrilla group, led by Salvador Sanchez Ceren, was founded in 1980 and recognized as a legal political party in 1992. FMLN is a socialist party and holds the mayor's office in the capital, San Salvador, and in other major cities, such as Santa Ana.

Alfredo Cristiani and his rightwing ARENA party governed El Salvador from 1989 to 1994.

PCN (Party of National Conciliation): With Ciro Cruz Zepeda as its leader, this small conservative party captured 16 seats in the 2003 legislative elections.

PDC (Christian Democratic Party): Rodolfo Parker led PDC in the 2003 elections as part of a coalition with smaller parties, capturing five seats.

ELECTIONS

The 1994 presidential, legislative, and municipal elections were significant in many ways. It is rare for all three elections to be held concurrently, but more importantly, they were the first to be held since civil war ended and the first to be open to the FMLN guerrilla group, now recognized as a legal party. The elections were seen as a test of the ability of a civilian government to hold its own against the military. Although it lost the

A crowd gathers to listen to a speaker in San Salvador's Central Plaza.

PEOPLE IN POLITICS, PAST AND PRESENT

JOSÉ NAPOLEÓN DUARTE: Former leader of the moderate PDC, he was tortured and exiled by government forces in 1972 but later returned to El Salvador and served as president from 1984 to 1989.

ROBERTO D'AUBUISSON: Founder of the rightwing ARENA party, he also set up the country's notorious death squads. He planned the 1980 assassination of Archbishop Oscar Arnulfo Romero.

ALFREDO CRISTIANI: Cristiani brought the rightwing ARENA party to power in 1989 and served as president until 1994. He ushered El Salvador into the postwar period.

RUBÉN ZAMORA *(right)*: This leftwing intellectual ran for president in the 1994 elections with the support of Democratic Convergence, a coalition of leftwing parties that included FMLN.

FRANCISCO FLORES PEREZ: This politician defeated FMLN's Facundo Guardado and won the presidential seat for ARENA in 1999. The pro-business politician adopted the U.S. dollar as the Salvadoran currency in January 2001. This reduced interest rates but increased inflation.

ANTONIO ELÍAS SACA: This rightwing politician started out as a television and radio sports commentator. Now owner of a radio network, Saca was sworn in as El Salvador's president for a five-year term in June 2004.

elections, FMLN established itself as the major opposition party.

During the legislative elections in 2003, the FMLN captured the largest number of votes—31 percent. FMLN's success concerned the U.S. government because the party was still seen as a threat to liberal capitalism. The U.S. government hinted that should the FMLN rule, it would withdraw aid and investments to El Salvador. In March 2004 ARENA's Antonio Elías Saca won the presidential elections with 57 percent of the votes.

ECONOMY

THE SALVADORAN ECONOMY has been based on agriculture for thousands of years, but when the Spanish colonists pushed the Indians off their small communal farms and used the land to grow cash crops, they made a fundamental change to the economy. Cash crops were indeed a success, and the later diversification into a greater variety of crops and into manufacturing ensured continued high levels of economic growth and extreme wealth for the few large landowners. The uneven distribution of wealth resulted in long-term political instability and, eventually, civil war. The war, in turn, had a major impact on the economy, causing a massive outflow of money, the destruction of much of the country's infrastructure, a decrease in exports, investment, and consumption, and even higher levels of unemployment. The peace accord brought generous foreign aid and the return of capital from abroad, restoring economic growth.

Left: **A bus in San Salvador is the target of economic sabotage. In the 1980s rebel forces believed that destroying urban infrastructure was the most effective way of putting pressure on the government to improve the economy.**

Opposite: **A Salvadoran farmer prepares coffee beans for drying. Coffee is an important crop to the country.**

President Francisco Flores Perez introduced the U.S. dollar into the Salvadoran economy in January 2001 to reduce domestic interest rates, exchange rate risk, and transaction costs for firms. The move is a reflection of the importance of the U.S. dollar in El Salvador—remittances from the United States are a substantial component of the Salvadoran economy.

El Salvador's public debt decreased from about 50 percent of the gross domestic product (GDP) in 1992 to about 30 percent in 2000. However, rebuilding and reconstruction efforts that followed Hurricane Mitch in 1998 and, particularly, the earthquakes in 2001 increased public debt to 43.7 percent in 2003.

Subsistence cattle herding supplements the food imported into the country.

Despite economic growth and relative stability, 48 percent of the population still live below the poverty line. Economic benefits have not been evenly shared across the different levels of the population.

AGRICULTURE

El Salvador's wealth was built on the export of just three crops: cacao, indigo, and coffee. This reliance on monocrops could not continue, however, as it made the Salvadoran economy extremely vulnerable to fluctuations in the economies of its trading partners. El Salvador diversified its agricultural exports into cotton, sugar, corn, rice, sorghum, beans, oilseed, and beef and dairy products.

COFFEE

Coffee has a long history that is shrouded in legend. First cultivated about A.D. 575, it was not grown extensively until the 15th century. By the 16th and 17th centuries, coffee consumption had spread throughout Persia and Turkey, continental Europe, England, and America. Europeans were in love with the drink. Coffeehouses sprang up everywhere and became popular social, literary, and political gathering places; King Charles II saw them as centers of dissent and tried, unsuccessfully, to shut them down.

Coffee grows wild in some parts of Ethiopia, where it originated, but is now cultivated wherever its needs for a hot and moist climate, rich soil, and a high altitude are met.

El Salvador has an ideal climate for coffee, but it was not until synthetic dyes made indigo unprofitable in the mid-1800s that the country began to direct its resources toward the large-scale production of coffee beans. This entailed putting the large peasant population to work on the plantations, laying the roads and railroads necessary for transporting the crop, and building processing plants.

In 1990 coffee prices crashed as a result of the overproduction of coffee worldwide. In 1993 El Salvador participated in the Coffee Retention Plan, which was an agreement among the world's coffee exporters to limit coffee production and thus boost prices. That, however, did not stop coffee from declining in importance in the Salvadoran economy. In 1987 coffee accounted for half of the export earnings; this decreased to 45 percent in the mid-1990s and dropped to only 7 percent in 2004.

Although coffee's role in the Salvadoran economy has diminished, it continues to provide El Salvador with a dependable export income.

The structure of the Salvadoran economy has changed considerably, and in 2003 agriculture as a whole accounted for only 9.4 percent of the country's GDP. This is in contrast to the situation in 1987, when it made up 25 percent of the GDP. Nevertheless, agriculture is still an important component of the economy and provides employment to 30 percent of the labor force.

LAND REFORM This has been a thorny issue in El Salvador for over a hundred years. Many attempts to redistribute land from the few large landowners to the majority of landless peasants have ended either in failure or in only partial success, contributing to the country's long history of poverty and violence.

Land reform was a key condition of the 1992 peace accord. The World Bank provided loans to El Salvador in 1996 and 2005, but despite international financial aid, land redistribution has been slow and inefficient due to such factors as the plummeting prices of cash crops, particularly coffee, bad weather, and regional economics.

Peace led to a mini-boom in construction, which enjoyed further growth due to reconstruction efforts following the 2001 earthquakes.

CONSTRUCTION

Since the 1992 peace accord, the return of capital, private investment, and national reconstruction programs have brought about growth in the construction industry. It was the leading sector in 2001 with a growth rate of 10 percent, due in part to the post-earthquake reconstruction projects. In the same year the construction sector employed 5.4 percent of the workforce and accounted for 3.9 percent of the GDP.

MANUFACTURING

El Salvador's manufacturing sector experienced rapid growth during the 1960s, but suffered a drastic decline during the 1980s when the civil war caused a shortage of capital and foreign currency, guerrilla sabotage of electrical power plants and factories, protests by labor unions, and reduced demand for products both at home and abroad. Nevertheless, the sector has managed to get back on track. In 2004 manufacturing accounted for 24 percent of the GDP, and between 1996 and 2003 it employed an almost constant rate of about 18 percent of the workforce. Apparel manufacturing lead the manufacturing sector's performance. Clothing and textiles, and products such as medicine, soap, iron, steel, and machinery generate more foreign earnings for El Salvador than do agricultural exports.

TRANSPORTATION AND UTILITIES

During the war much of El Salvador's infrastructure was severely damaged by guerrilla forces. Peace has brought pledges of financial support from around the world for the reconstruction of major highways, power plants, electrical towers, and telecommunications facilities. El Salvador privatized its telecommunication services in 1996, and today the market is one of the most liberalized in the region. There is one telephone line for every nine people with several companies offering fixed and mobile telecommunication services. Internet connectivity is available in El Salvador, and in 2003 there were over half a million Internet users in the country.

The industrial sector as a whole accounted for 31.2 percent of the GDP in 2003.

El Salvador depends on imported oil for its energy needs. Since the oil price shocks of 1973 and 1979, when the world supply of petroleum was drastically reduced, El Salvador has tried to decrease its dependence on imported petroleum by developing alternative forms of energy. Renewable energy sources, such as hydroelectric plants, solid and liquid biomass, and geothermal energy provide almost half of the country's energy needs.

MONEY FROM ABROAD

El Salvador relies heavily on remittances and foreign aid, which, along with the return of private investment capital, has increased since peace was negotiated in 1992.

An electrical repairman. During the civil war, the FMLN damaged almost every power plant in El Salvador and destroyed more than 1,000 high-tension electrical towers.

Driven by poverty, as many as 3 million Salvadorans are estimated to be living and working abroad, especially in the United States. They send money home every month. Such remittances totalled $2.5 billion in 2004, or 17.1 percent of the Salvadoran GDP, one of the highest rates in the world. Despite the large amount, remittance money is only sufficient for purchasing basic items, such as food and clothing, in El Salvador. Post-war economic policies, such as the dollarization plan backed by the International Monetary Fund (IMF), privatization, and huge tax breaks for large corporations, have almost doubled the cost of living for the average Salvadoran. Now, more than before, Salvadorans are desperately depending on remittances by family members working abroad.

At a private satellite television station in San Salvador members of a Salvadoran family react as they join in a video conference with relatives who have emigrated to the United States. Thousands of Salvadorans fled to the United States during their country's civil war. In 2004 Salvadorans abroad sent home $2.5 billion in remittances.

ENVIRONMENT

PROBLEMS WITH EL SALVADOR'S environment, particularly deforestation, have their roots deep in social, political, and economic inequalities, which can be traced all the way back to the colonial era. Colonists took land away from the locals and forced them to work on plantations. In successive centuries the landowning elite worked hand in hand with the authorities to ensure that the majority of the population remained landless farmers. The 1980s land reforms were unsuccessful because the farmers were given land that was infertile. The signing of peace agreements in 1992 allowed the government to refocus and better manage its heavily depleted resources. Progress, however, has been slow.

Above: **A worker harvests red ripe coffee beans on a plantation. Many forests in El Salvador were cleared to make way for large coffee plantations.**

Opposite: **Isla de Pajaros, or Bird Island, in Palo Verde National Park is home to such birds as spoonbills, egrets, ibis, and herons.**

DEFORESTATION

Deforestation is the main environmental concern for El Salvador, which has a total forest area of 299,000 acres (121,000 hectares), or only 5.8 percent of the land. The forest area declined 37 percent between 1990 and 2000 alone. Many of the forests have made way for large coffee plantations and other agricultural projects by wealthy landowners. The trees were also destroyed in the civil war or cut for firewood by rural Salvadorans. Adding to the problem are overpopulation, which means more and more land is needed for building residences, and indiscriminate slashing and burning of trees to clear farmland for cultivation.

The absence of trees leaves the topsoil vulnerable to erosion, which leaches the soil of its fertility. Deforestation also leads to a lower amount of transpiration, which dries out the air. Temperatures increase and the amount of rainfall decreases as a result. Water bodies dry up, and more people do not have access to sufficient clean water. This, combined with declining crop yields due to the poor quality of the soil, affects Salvadorans' lives and livelihood.

The country's species biodiversity has suffered as a direct result of deforestation. Many species of plants and animals, such as the jaguar and scarlet macaw, have become extinct. Some migratory birds from North America are deprived of their transit nests in El Salvador during their journey south in the winter.

MANGROVE MANAGEMENT

Forests in the coastal areas and wetlands are not spared from exploitation. Without access to electricity, rural residents living along coastal areas

NATIONAL RECONCILIATION FOREST

Twelve years of civil war in El Salvador took more than 75,000 lives and caused widespread damage. It was estimated that areas surrounding Guazapa Mountain alone were pounded with 4,000 tons of napalm and white phosphorus bombs. These caused huge craters in the mountainside, and the resulting fires wiped out much of the forest. By the end of the war, bare ridges and stretches of dry riverbeds replaced what used to be dense canopies of greenery and clear, flowing rivers.

In 1996 the people of Guazapa launched a project to convert much of the bare mountain soil into what was called the National Reconciliation Forest. The project involved planting 75,000 trees, one for each person killed in the civil war, high on the volcanic slopes of Guazapa Mountain. On the lower slopes they planted trees for timber and fuel. To the people there, the simple logic of "more trees, more water, more animals, more fertile lands" drives them to take responsibility for helping the mountain recover. Apart from restoring the forest and rebuilding the ecosystem, the project also educates farmers on sustainable agricultural practices.

cut trees in mangrove forests for firewood. Mostly shrimp farmers, these Salvadorans living in the coastal areas do not realize that the destruction of mangrove forests may affect their very livelihood. Aquatic wildlife, such as shellfish and shrimp, have been affected by the reduction in mangrove forests. There is also worry that excessive farming of shrimp may upset the ecological balance in mangroves. Mangroves are important in preventing coastal erosion and to some extent provide some protection to the coast against destructive tidal waves.

These Salvadoran children look for mollusks in a mangrove swamp to help supplement their family's meager earnings.

GULF OF FONSECA

An important coastal formation on the Pacific side of Central America is the Gulf of Fonseca, which is shared by El Salvador, Honduras, and Nicaragua. It covers 700 square miles (1,800 square km) of aquatic area and is home to more than 1.5 million people.

Some communities along the Gulf have poor natural resources and substandard living conditions. The population is rapidly increasing, and the wetlands of the Gulf of Fonseca are threatened by the population's exploitation of the natural resources.

Commercial shrimp farming is the main culprit in the destruction of the mangroves and their ecosystem in the gulf. To get rid of organisms that threaten the development of shrimp larvae, shrimp farmers use toxic chemicals, which also poison other fauna in the area. Dumping of solid waste, sewage water, and industrial toxic waste into the water adds to the pollution in the gulf. The use of mangrove wood as fuel directly results in shrinking mangrove forests.

Most communities in the area have no sanitary landfills or garbage dumps. Over 50 percent of the population uses outdoor latrines, and over 90 percent of the population throws garbage into rivers and marshes. Health services are inadequate, and more than 15 percent of children born in this area die before turning 5 years old.

The World Conservation Union (IUCN) has stepped in to move the three governments into action to prevent further deterioration of the gulf's condition. They have intervened with sustainable management programs for the gulf, which include building infrastructure for human habitation. People living in the Gulf of Fonseca are educated on environmental issues so that they can participate in resource conservation. Studies are also being conducted on how to practice fishing and shrimp cultivation in a sustainable way.

Stricter enforcement by environmental organizations, such as the Gulf of Fonseca Committee for the Defense and Sustainable Development of Flora and Fauna, as well as the Central American Water Tribunal, is giving hope to the gulf. However, observers have commented that these efforts are not moving at the same speed as the population expansion and the accompanying exploitation of natural resources.

URBAN POLLUTION

Poverty and overpopulation remain the primary cause of environmental degradation. About 63 percent of Salvadorans live in urban areas, particularly San Salvador, Santa Ana, and San Miguel. The city of San Salvador is home to almost one-quarter of El Salvador's population.

Overcrowding and the absence of proper sanitation are the main culprits of air, water, and solid waste pollution. There is heavy traffic on the roads, and poorly maintained vehicles emit thick black smoke. The smoke remains in the air because it is trapped by the surrounding hills and mountains.

In terms of housing, there is still a disparity between the rich few and the poor masses. The latter live mostly in makeshift houses in areas without a municipal sewage system. They dispose of solid waste in their backyards, rivers, and streams. With the rapidly growing urban population, it is an uphill task for Salvadorans to resolve the environmental crisis.

INTERVENTION AND CONSERVATION EFFORTS

Environmental issues became a priority during the reconstruction of post-war El Salvador. A presidential decree created the Ministry of Environment and Natural Resources (MARN) in 1997 to better manage the country's resources. The ministry coordinates efforts by the government and non-governmental organizations (NGOs) in the area of environmental conservation. It is also responsible for recommending environmental legislation and enforcing

Vehicles that use diesel, such as this bus, contribute to air pollution in El Salvador.

Birdwatching in El Impossible National Park in San Salvador.

existing ones in El Salvador. Apart from environmental rehabilitation, MARN has established the National Protected Areas System (SANP), which marks geographical areas of concern according to such categories as national parks, national monuments, habitat or species management areas, and marine and terrestrial landscapes.

In the international arena, El Salvador participates in a number of conservation projects and is a signatory of a number of conventions, such as the Convention on International Trade in Endangered Species of Wild Fauna and Flora (1987) and the Convention on Biological Diversity (1994). El Salvador is a participant in the United States Agency for International Development's (USAID) Tropical Forest Conservation Act, which was enacted in 1998.

El Salvador is also involved in the Mesoamerican Biological Corridor, which is a project that seeks to protect ecosystems in the region. Several international organizations, such as the World Bank, United Nations Environment Program (UNEP), and the Global Environment Facility, provide funding for this large and complex project. It employs a multi-pronged approach to conservation, such as relocating communities out of ecologically fragile areas.

International funding and participation in projects such as the above have facilitated MARN's efforts in reforestation, management of natural areas, wildlife conservation, and management of solid waste. Although faced with a few setbacks, such as Hurricane Mitch in 1998 and a series of devastating earthquakes in 2001, environmental rehabilitation in El Salvador is well under way. One major challenge that the government must overcome to ensure future environmental sustainability in the long run will be the eradication of poverty and the management of overpopulation.

Laguna Verde, or Green Lagoon, is a volcanic crater lake located in the Ahuachapan Province.

SALVADORANS

THE ORIGINAL PEOPLE of what is now El Salvador were a network of Mayan Indian tribes who inhabited the region for thousands of years. Their descendants, the Pipil Indians, lived in the area when the Spanish arrived in the 16th century, but disease, persecution, and intermarriage led to their gradual elimination.

Today 90 percent of the Salvadoran population is mestizo—of mixed Indian and Spanish descent. Ladino is another term that is often used in Latin America; it applies to any person—whether of European, Indian, or mestizo descent—who speaks Spanish and is Westernized.

The population in El Salvador is largely homogenous ethnically and linguistically, but it is sharply divided between the rich and the poor. Most of the country's wealth lies in the hands of just 2 percent of the population. At least 48 percent of Salvadorans live below the poverty line, and the majority work long hours on plantations, in factories, or in the military for very low wages. A small percentage have achieved middle-class status by becoming teachers, doctors, civil servants, or business people, or by rising through the ranks of the military.

Opposite: **A little girl is dressed for a procession.**

Below: **A truck driver naps in a hammock attached to the side of his truck.**

DESCENDANTS OF THE PIPIL INDIANS

In the 1800s Indians made up 60 percent of the population. Today they form just 1 percent of the nation.

Only 1 percent of Salvadorans are descendants of the Pipil Indians, who inhabited El Salvador before the arrival of the Spanish. Primarily Pancho and Izalco Indians, they live in a cluster of villages in southwestern El Salvador near the Guatemalan border. Their elaborate ceremonial costumes are reserved for special occasions, but some Indian women still wear a version of the traditional skirt with plain white or brightly colored blouses. Only a few elders still speak their native Nahua language. Although the government and the Jesuit-run University of Central America attempted to revive the Nahua language and Indian customs in the 1970s, Indians shied away from the effort once civil war broke out. A long history of persecution at the hands of the government and the oligarchy has resulted in many Indians refusing even to teach Nahua to their children.

A smiling old Indian man in Chalchuapa. Although a few Indians still wear traditional clothes, most have adopted a ladino lifestyle and wear Western-style dress.

THE OLIGARCHY

Salvadorans of direct European descent make up only 1 percent of the population, yet this small white minority has—directly or indirectly—controlled the country's power and wealth for almost 500 years. The oligarchy's lifestyle is much the same as that of wealthy people in any other big, modern, cosmopolitan city: they wear designer clothes, drive luxury cars, and vacation abroad. Even within this elite there is a hierarchy. At the top of the pyramid are the families of the "founding fathers"—the original Spanish settlers of El Salvador; next are the descendants of the bankers and financiers who immigrated from various parts of Europe in the 19th and early 20th centuries; at the bottom are the newly rich Palestinians, Lebanese, and Jews, who make up the merchant class. The upper class also includes the officer ranks of the military, although the oligarchy and military remain separate entities and tend not to mix socially.

A maid accompanies the daughter of a wealthy family to a private school in San Salvador.

59

Right: **A poor family of farm hands. Nearly half of the rural population is landless, and very few of those who do own their own land can grow enough food for their families—the soil is too poor and the plots are too small.**

Below: **Some urban Salvadorans are so destitute that they are forced to make a living—and sometimes their home—on the cities' garbage dumps.**

THE MIDDLE CLASS

Making up only about 8 percent of the population, El Salvador's middle class includes professional and skilled workers, government employees, school teachers, and small landowners. Although the middle class has tended to encourage land reform and push for an improvement in the standard of

Middle-class teenagers enjoy a day out.

living of most Salvadorans, they have had little direct influence in the country's affairs. Many teachers, doctors, and trade unionists were politically active during the war and frequently became the targets of political military harassment and violence.

LANDLESS PEASANTS AND URBAN POOR

Whether they live in the city or in the countryside, most mestizo and Indian Salvadorans are poor and unemployed. They try to eke out a living by working on plantations, in factories, or in the military. Agricultural work is seasonal, so even farm workers are out of work for part of the year. Thousands of people flock to the cities each year in search of work, despite the disheartening fact that urban unemployment is high. They do whatever they can to get by, living in makeshift huts and selling fruit and vegetables on the streets.

Refugees in Usulután line up for a simple meal of beans and tortillas. Many less fortunate refugees starved during the war.

REFUGEES

During the civil war some 2 million Salvadorans fled to the United States, Mexico, and other Central American countries. Half of these Salvadorans sought refuge in the United States alone; their remittances helped to boost El Salvador's economy. Many live in the United States illegally and work in temporary, low-paying jobs, such as babysitting, gardening, cleaning, and dog-walking.

Few Salvadorans have been granted political asylum. Many U.S. courts were reluctant to accept that Salvadorans were fleeing political violence rather than simply seeking out a better life, as this acknowledgment would have made it difficult for the United States to justify continuing its financial and military support of the war in El Salvador.

Even though many Salvadorans do not receive political asylum, a 1986 U.S. amnesty law granted legal status to immigrants that entered the United States before 1982. In 1992 Salvadorans who had been in the United States since 1990 received a Temporary Protected Status (TPS), which allows them to live and work in the country. The TPS was offered again to Salvadorans following the 2001 earthquakes in El Salvador.

In Central America, refugee camps were set up to shelter Salvadorans who fled the civil war. Several large refugee groups have returned home from the countries they fled to and formed new settlements, or repatriation communities, on the sites of villages destroyed during the war. As a tribute, several of these communities were christened with the names of priests who were killed in the war.

CIUDAD ROMERO The community of Ciudad Romero is a community that serves as a shining example of the perseverance and community spirit of Salvadorans in the face of decades of poverty, suffering, and repression. One such example is Ciudad Romero.

In May 1980 some Salvadorans fled their village in La Unión after it was subjected to bombing and persecution. The group of refugees left El Salvador on foot, traveled through Honduras, and finally settled on the east coast of Panama. There they established a new community called Ciudad Romero, in honor of the revered Archbishop Oscar Arnulfo Romero, who had been assassinated in El Salvador earlier that year. In Ciudad Romero they built a chapel and a school, and began to cultivate crops of corn, cacao, and rice. Despite their complete isolation from other communities, which meant that they were unable to sell their crops or buy medicine and other necessities, their community continued to grow.

In January 1991 the people of Ciudad Romero were allowed to return home to El Salvador after a long process of negotiation with the Salvadoran government. It took a great deal of support from grassroots organizations and the Catholic Church in El Salvador, but eventually the refugees established their new settlement in the department of Usulután, in eastern El Salvador. There they built basic infrastructure, such as a school, cooperative store, and communal kitchen. The people rear pigs, chickens, and cattle and work on their plot of land for subsistence.

LIFESTYLE

SALVADORANS are a very sociable, hardworking, devout, and generous people, despite considerable hardship and adversity. Friends and family are central to daily life, although migration due to unemployment and civil war has broken apart many families and communities. Poverty abounds in El Salvador, and malnutrition is a serious problem, affecting one in every five children. Since most pregnant women are undernourished themselves, many children start life with serious nutritional deficiencies.

The lifestyle of the poor in El Salvador, whether in rural areas or in the cities, revolves around providing food and shelter for the family, and there is little time for leisure or education, or money for the modern conveniences that would make life easier and more pleasurable. Wealthier Salvadorans, on the other hand, own cars, work in office buildings, shop in malls, and live in modern houses.

Left: **A "traffic clown" brightens up the day by directing traffic in San Salvador.**

Opposite: **A Salvadoran woman sells flowers at a market in Cuscatlán.**

RURAL LIFE

A young mother carries home firewood. Most rural houses are without electricity, so cooking is done over a wood or charcoal fire.

About half of all Salvadorans live in rural areas. The vast majority of them work for large landowners at an hourly wage that cannot pay for adequate food for their families. Houses are small and very basic, transportation is generally by foot or by horse and cart, and long hours are spent getting through the day's work and household chores. At harvest time, the whole family works in the fields. Illiteracy is high, as children leave school at an early age to work or help out at home.

As most houses have no running water or electricity, rural Salvadorans use wood or charcoal to cook by fire, and burn candles or kerosene lamps for light. Water is usually collected from rivers and streams, even though the surface water is seriously polluted by agricultural and industrial waste. Because of the widespread danger of cholera, most people have developed the practice of disinfecting the water by adding bleach.

THE WORKLOAD OF A RURAL WOMAN

A typical day for a rural woman begins before dawn. The first task is to fetch water, which may be as far as an hour's walk away. When she gets back, she gathers firewood, builds a fire, and makes the day's supply of tortillas. On top of buying food at the daily market, cooking, washing clothes in the river, cleaning the house, and caring for the children, her tasks include tending the garden and raising chickens and pigs. During the harvest season, she works on the farm alongside her husband, often without pay. She might also try to earn extra money for the family by selling vegetables, homemade fruit drinks, or candles in the local market or at a roadside stand.

Most Salvadoran women wash clothes in rivers or lakes because they do not have running water at home.

Modern San Salvador.

LIFE IN THE CITY

Almost a third of El Salvador's population lives in the capital city of San Salvador. The downtown streets are congested with cars, buses, street vendors, and pedestrians, and the air is thick with pollution. Most urban Salvadorans work in factories, offices, and shops or as domestic workers. They shop at large central markets or modern, multistory shopping centers. The wide disparity between rich and poor is especially evident in San Salvador. The wealthy live in quiet, elegant suburbs, socialize in private clubs, dine in fine restaurants, and shop in expensive boutiques, while the poor live in slums on the edge of the city, getting by as best as they can.

HOUSING

RURAL The most common kind of house, the *choza* (CHO-sah), is made of woven branches and covered with mud. Others are made of adobe, or sun-dried mud bricks, which are sometimes whitewashed. Houses have dirt floors and thatched or tiled roofs, and few have running water or electricity. Living quarters are typically crowded, with six or more people living in one or two rooms that are divided by curtains rather than walls. Family members pull out cots, hammocks, or straw mats to sleep on at night.

URBAN The wealthy live in modern houses with swimming pools, well-tended gardens, and elaborate security systems. The small middle-class population live in row houses or in comfortable apartments, either inside the city or in the suburbs. Most of the poor live in *tugurios* (tu-GU-ryos), shantytowns made of tin or cardboard, with dirt floors, no electricity, and no access to running water or sewage services, while others rent rooms in crowded, rundown buildings called *mesones* (may-SON-ays)—chains of tiny, often windowless rooms surrounding a common courtyard, with a common latrine but no washing or cooking facilities.

Salvadorans flock to the capital city of San Salvador in search of work and a better way of life, but many of them end up living in shantytowns such as this one.

Salvadorans collecting water from a well. Inferior sanitation and the scarcity of safe drinking water are major causes of illness and disease in El Salvador.

HEALTH CARE

Health care is a problem for the majority of Salvadorans. Medical facilities are inadequate, especially in rural areas. Most of the few hospitals that exist are overcrowded, rundown, and badly equipped, and facilities are often insanitary. Hospital patients are usually advised to bring their own food, bedsheets, soap, toilet paper, and even surgical supplies. The shortage of medical facilities often means that only patients needing emergency surgery receive treatment, while non-urgent cases have to wait.

Qualified doctors and nurses are in short supply. In 1989 the Ministry of Planning in El Salvador reported that there were only 12 hospital beds, 3.2 doctors, and 2.1 nurses for every 10,000 people. This improved by 2000—there were 52 beds and 26.5 doctors for every 10,000 people, although more than 60 percent of medical personnel were based in the capital. The country's health care sector suffered a major setback as a result of the 2001 earthquakes, which severely damaged 55 percent of hospitals and other health care facilities.

Poor sanitation and a lack of access to safe drinking water, especially among rural dwellers, cause a high number of deaths from waterborne diseases such as diarrhea and gastroenteritis. A 2000 survey by the Pan American Health Organization (PAHO) indicated that only 12 percent of ill Salvadorans seek medical care. Most illnesses are treated with traditional remedies or left unattended.

Malnutrition, resulting from an inadequate consumption of calories and protein, is another leading cause of death in both adults and children. Illnesses due to vitamin and nutrition deficiencies are common in El Salvador. The 12-year civil war only made it harder for Salvadorans to find adequate and nutritious food for themselves and their families. Between 1998 and 2003, 13 percent of babies were born underweight, often to women who lacked proper nourishment themselves.

Certain agricultural practices, including the use of pesticides and herbicides in farming, cause such illnesses as respiratory problems, heart disease, and malformed babies. Because a considerable amount of the land in El Salvador is used for agriculture, this problem is a pervasive one.

Adult life expectancy, however, has improved in El Salvador over the past two decades. In 1985 the life expectancy for men was 59 years and for women, 68 years. Between 1990 and 1995 this increased to 63 years for men and 71 for women. The life expectancy in El Salvador continues to improve—the average male baby born in 2004 can expect to live until the age of 67 years, and the average female baby until the age of 75. Nevertheless, these figures still lag behind those of the United States, where the average man is expected to live up to 74.6 years of age and up to 80.3 years for women.

There was a massive outbreak of diarrhea and gastroenteritis in El Salvador just prior to the 2001 earthquakes.

THE FAMILY

Traditionally the family is central to life in El Salvador, and families tend to be large, due partly to the dominance of Roman Catholicism, which is against contraception, and partly through necessity. In rural areas, especially, women are urged to marry young and have several children. Children are considered an economic asset. They are relied upon to help earn income for the family and to care for their parents in their old age.

Family unity is important, and extended families are common, with three generations often living under the same roof. Upper-class families are tied to one another by a complex web of marriage and kinship. This is one of the ways in which they have managed to hold on to their power and wealth.

Approximately 37 percent of El Salvador's population consists of people who are 14 years of age and below.

Women head many Salvadoran families.

Most births take place alone with the mother cutting the cord and burying the placenta, a Salvadoran tradition. Physician-assisted deliveries occur only in complicated pregnancies or emergency situations. The high birth rate is a way of compensating for the high infant mortality rate—many rural children die in their first year from disease or malnutrition.

The influence of Catholicism broadened the concept of family to include *padrinos* (pa-DREE-nos, or godfathers) and *madrinas* (ma-DREE-nas, or godmothers). Godparents played an important role in a child's upbringing. Today, however, the practice of godparenting is less widespread.

Family support has helped poor people endure the years of poverty and hardship, although civil war and chronic unemployment have taken their toll on family unity. Although Salvadoran society is traditionally patriarchal, as is the case in most of Latin America, many rural families are in fact headed by women, as the men left home in search of work or became casualties of the war. Common-law marriages and free unions are common in rural areas.

Many women joined the guerrilla forces during the war. Men and women were treated as equals— women shared in the fighting and men shared in the cooking.

THE POSITION OF WOMEN

Women in El Salvador have faced widespread exploitation and oppression due to the circumstances of poverty, war, or simply tradition. Domestic abuse by fathers and husbands is common. Machismo, the Latin American ideal of manliness, dictates that men are superior to women, that a husband should earn the money for his family, and that the wife should do the "women's work" of cooking, cleaning, and caring for the children. The economic reality in El Salvador, however, is that most families require two income-earning parents. The social reality is that many men abandon their wives, leaving approximately one-quarter of all households headed by women.

Guerrilla groups tried to overcome the widespread attitude of women as inferior beings. In the areas they controlled during the war, they discouraged wife-beating and stressed the equality of women in almost every aspect of work. Men and women shared responsibility for cooking, washing clothes, and working on construction and development projects.

Many Salvadoran women themselves have started to act as a force for positive change, forming organizations to tackle some of the fundamental issues that have prevented women from achieving equality, especially in rural areas. Such issues include the lack of education, high infant mortality rate, and high birth rate. These organizations provide a broad range of services, such as medical, legal, educational, childcare, family planning, and job placement.

The government has passed laws granting women equal legal status and "equal pay for equal work," but in practice many women still face discrimination in the workplace and are usually paid only half the salary that a man earns for the same work.

Landowners often refuse to pay women for their labor.

EDUCATION

The government provides free education up to grade nine, but many children, __ ally in the rural areas, do not attend school because the cost of supplies, transportation, school uniforms, and matriculation fee are too expensive for many poor families. This problem is compounded by a shortage of teachers and schools, and many children have to leave school after only a year or two in order to help support their family by working on plantations. With the government committed to enforcing compulsory education, international agencies, such as World Bank and

Salvadoran children in an outdoor study session.

the United States Agency for International Development (USAID), launched several programs to make education accessible to Salvadoran children in the rural areas.

A year before the signing of the peace agreements, the World Bank piloted a community-managed education program, or EDUCO, in rural El Salvador. Positive results achieved during the trial period led to the program being expanded throughout the country in a 10-year plan launched in 1995. EDUCO aims to increase student enrollment and teacher attendance, better administration of schools, and promoting parents' understanding of the importance of education for their children.

In 2003 USAID and the Salvadoran Ministry of Education launched an Excellence in Classroom Education at the Local Level (EXCELL). Targeted at principals, teachers, and school managers, the program was designed to address educational priorities and improve educational performance of children in 250 rural elementary schools in El Salvador. These collaborative efforts display clear commitment by the government to improve the quality of education, particularly in rural parts of the country.

A statue at a San Salvador university is riddled by bullets. Campuses were hotbeds of activism during the civil war and prime targets of military crackdowns.

TRANSPORTATION

El Salvador has more than 7,440 miles (12,000 km) of roads as well as two major highways (the Pan American Highway and the Carretora Litoral) that run the length of the country. These roads, however, are more likely to be traveled by buses and trucks than by private cars. A considerable number of roads were damaged by earthquakes in 2001, and the government began repair works in the same year.

Taxis are plentiful in the capital city of San Salvador, but most Salvadorans get around by bus, bicycle, or on foot. In rural areas, horses are another common form of transportation. The bus system is extensive and is the most popular method of traveling long distances.

Ferrocarriles Nacionales de El Salvador (FENADESAL), the national railway, is responsible for several hundred miles of railroad. The railway is used mainly for carrying goods and cargo, such as iron, cement, and dairy products. Like the roads, half of the railroad system was damaged by earthquakes in recent years, and El Salvador is working on the repairs.

The international airport near San Salvador is one of the most modern in the region and is served by a number of international airlines. Transportes Aéreos Centroamericanos (TACA), El Salvador's privately owned national airline, flies passengers to all Central American capital cities, Mexico City, and most major U.S. cities.

SHOPPING

In San Salvador, the most popular shopping places are the central market and Metrocentro, a modern, split-level shopping mall offering a wide variety of goods in air-conditioned boutiques. Metrocentro is reputed to be the largest shopping mall in Central America. In smaller towns and villages, open-air markets and general stores stock a limited range of basic goods, such as clothing, food, and household goods.

EATING OUT

Dining out in one of San Salvador's many upscale restaurants is a luxury that few ordinary Salvadorans can afford, but there are many popular alternatives offering a quick and inexpensive bite to eat. Small restaurants, sidewalk vendors, and market kitchens sell a variety of local specialties. American fast-food chain restaurants can also be found in the capital city of San Salvador.

Below: **A boutique in San Salvador's Metrocentro shopping mall sells imported clothing.**

Bottom: **Small restaurants like this one abound in El Salvador. Most serve stuffed tortillas, a Salvadoran specialty that is very time-consuming to make at home.**

79

RELIGION

THE STRONGEST RELIGIONS in El Salvador today are Roman Catholicism and evangelical Protestantism. Like much of Latin America, El Salvador is an intensely religious society— even non-practicing Catholics and people not affiliated with any religion say they pray at least once a day.

Roman Catholicism was brought to Latin America as part of the Spanish conquest, and it has played an extremely important role in shaping the culture of the region. In El Salvador, the Catholic Church generally supported the ruling classes and the social and economic systems that caused much hardship for the majority of Salvadorans. Even so, 83 percent of Salvadorans are Catholic. Church rituals and symbols have permeated society, and Catholicism's traditions of community, hierarchy, and social and family ties remain strong.

Membership in other religious denominations, including Baha'is, Evangelicals, Mormons, Seventh-Day Adventists, and Jehovah's Witnesses, is increasing, and gradually eroding the dominance of Roman Catholicism. Evangelical church services provide a supportive and charismatic environment that is particularly appealing to large numbers of Salvadorans who are poor and displaced from their community. Liberation theology, a political offshoot of Roman Catholicism, is also popular in El Salvador.

Above: **A simple cross marks the grave of a Salvadoran peasant.**

Opposite: **Youths wearing ghoulish masks for a patron saint's festival stand in front of the Santa Lucia Church in Cuscatlán.**

CATHOLICISM

The dominance of Catholicism in El Salvador is demonstrated by the number of religious holidays and festivals that fill the Salvadoran calendar and the abundance of Catholic churches, symbols, and shrines throughout the country. Every town and Catholic church in El Salvador has a patron saint, who is honored annually with great pomp and festivity.

The biggest patron saint event is held during the first week of August, in homage to El Salvador del Mundo, or Savior of the World. Salvadorans celebrate by taking part in processions, fairs, carnival rides, and games. There are also lots of food and fireworks.

Despite its widespread popularity, Catholicism is beginning to lose its grip on many aspects of daily life. Both civil and religious marriage ceremonies are less prevalent in El Salvador than in other Latin American

The majestic Metropolitan Cathedral is a landmark in San Salvador.

CATHOLIC SHRINES

Catholic shrines in El Salvador attract pilgrims and visitors from far and wide. The Virgin Mary is a particularly important symbol, as it is in every Catholic society, and several outdoor shrines have been erected in her honor.

An elegant white shrine, La Ceiba de Guadalupe, stands in San Salvador in tribute to the Virgin of Guadalupe. December 12 is her celebration day.

The small town of Cojutepeque near San Salvador attracts a steady flow of pilgrims, especially on May 13. There, in a large park on the Hill of the Turkeys, is a shrine to the Virgin of Fátima. The Virgin Mary is said to have appeared to three Portuguese shepherd children on May 13, 1917, in Fátima, Portugal. The statue was brought to El Salvador from Fátima in 1949.

countries, and there is a relatively high rate of family breakdown. Divorces and common-law marriages are on the rise, and many children are born out of wedlock. Also, the practice of selecting godparents for children is becoming less widespread.

ABORTION El Salvador amended its constitution in 1999 to recognize that life begins at the moment of conception. This effectively bans abortions on any grounds. Critics say that the timing, just before elections, was to garner the votes of Catholics, who form the majority of the population.

THE INFLUENCE OF CATHOLICISM

Even though Catholicism in El Salvador is waning, the people still observe some formalities associated with the religion. For example, public holidays in El Salvador center on religious events, such as Christmas and Easter, and every town has a festival for its patron saint.

In the past, Salvadorans attached a lot of importance to the rites of passage. They christened and baptized their babies into the church. *Padrinos*, or godparents, were carefully chosen for each child and were given the responsibility of guiding the child's spiritual—and sometimes material—development. Entrance into adulthood during the child's 15th year was celebrated with a church ceremony called a *quinciñera* (keen-see-NYE-rah) *(above)*. Weddings were always formal occasions and usually took place in a church, and death was "celebrated" with a *vela* (VAY-lah), or wake.

Today, however, not all of these are commonly practiced by Salvadorans. Social and economic conditions have changed, particularly during and after the civil war.

CATHOLICISM'S LIBERATION THEOLOGY

In the late 1960s some members of the Roman Catholic Church in El Salvador were inspired by the Second Vatican Council's reforms on Catholicism and the Second Latin American Bishops' Conference's resolution on greater efforts to help the poor. They began saying Mass in Spanish instead of Latin and applying the Bible to contemporary problems. Priests and lay leaders began to work with the poor and tried to improve their quality of life physically as well as spiritually. People formed small groups called Christian Base Communities (CEB), which discussed how situations described in the Bible could be applied to their own lives, and started agitating for change.

As a result of this challenge to the existing social and political order, many members of the oligarchy and the military began to view the Church as subversive and Communist. Several church workers and members of CEBs became targets of violence.

Violence continued throughout the 1980s, causing so many priests to resign that nearly half of the rural parishes were left without one. Many of the CEBs dissolved or went underground, continuing their activities in secret. Many lay leaders of the CEBs joined the guerrillas, and some priests continued working in the conflict zones, trying to emphasize the need for social and political organization among the poor. Many were assassinated. The death of Archbishop Romero and other popular priests turned them into martyrs and added fire to the cause. The new archbishop, Arturo Rivera Damás, distanced himself and the Church hierarchy from the growing political struggle, but he served as a mediator in negotiations between the government and the insurgents. He died in 1995 and has since been replaced by Archbishop Fernando Saenz Lacalle. Liberation theology continued to have its mobilizing effect at the grassroots level.

Archbishop Romero spoke out against atrocities performed by the government and was seen to be in favor of liberation theology.

Archbishop Romero is believed to have made a radical shift away from conservatism after the assassination of his good friend Father Rutilio Grande. Father Rutilio was a Jesuit priest who believed in liberation theology and was outspoken in defense of the poor. When Father Rutilio was killed, Archbishop Romero felt he could no longer ignore the brutality of the government.

ARCHBISHOP ROMERO

Faced with the rise of liberation theology and a challenge to the status quo, in 1977 the Vatican appointed Oscar Arnulfo Romero to be the new archbishop and to reinforce a conservative authority in El Salvador.

As Archbishop Romero became familiar with the reality of life in El Salvador, however, he began to speak out against the widespread repression and poverty he saw. He encouraged workers to campaign for an increase in wages and a redistribution of land, and he called on the government to end repression and bring about social justice.

Within two years the small, soft-spoken, and bespectacled Archbishop Romero had become a much-loved figure among the ordinary people of El Salvador. But he was viewed as a major threat by the government and the military. Branded as a guerrilla, he was assassinated while celebrating Mass on March 24, 1980. The murder shocked people both inside and outside El Salvador and was one of the events that sparked the outbreak of civil war.

Although the government officially attributed the murder to unidentified members of rightwing death squads, Roberto d'Aubuisson, leader of the ARENA party, was widely believed to be responsible. At the end of the civil war 12 years later, the Truth Commission, mandated by the peace agreement to investigate the worst crimes of the war, found that d'Aubuisson had indeed ordered the murder of Archbishop Romero.

PROTESTANTS

Protestantism has enjoyed tremendous growth and has contributed to the decline of the Catholic Church in El Salvador. Evangelical missionaries, primarily from the United States, have become so influential that all non-Catholic groups working and preaching in Central America, including Presbyterians, Lutherans, Mormons, and Jehovah's Witnesses, are referred to as evangelicals.

Although evangelicals use some of the same techniques as liberation theologists, meeting in small groups and emphasizing prayer and personal responsibility, they generally discourage efforts to achieve social and political change and have thus won the support of the oligarchy and the military. On the other hand, some of the more mainstream Protestant groups, such as Baptists, Episcopalians, and Lutherans, espoused liberation theology and won many converts among the poor.

Inside an evangelical church. Protestantism emphasizes the direct relationship between an individual and God.

INDIAN RELIGION

The religion practiced by Indians in Central America has been described by anthropologists as Christo-pagan due to its complex mix of indigenous beliefs and the Christianity of early Roman Catholic missionaries.

Christian baptism, for example, is the first major event in the life of an individual, and a child is not considered fully human until the baptism has been performed. At the other end of the life cycle, the usual Christian rituals are observed. At funerals, the body is buried, church bells are rung, incense is burned, and prayers are read in church and at the graveside. Christian deities and saints have replaced the hierarchy of indigenous supernatural beings, but pagan beliefs remain. For example, disease is attributed to witchcraft or the failure to appease evil spirits.

A church in the Indian village of Panchimalco reflects the typical blend of indigenous and Christian influences.

THE INDIAN STORY OF CREATION

Indians in Central America believed that four worlds, or Suns, were created by gods and then destroyed by catastrophes before the present universe came into being.

According to the Aztec legend of creation, the first Sun was called Four-Jaguar and was destroyed by jaguars. At the end of the second Sun, Four-Wind, mankind was transformed into monkeys by a hurricane unleashed by the wind god. The god of thunder and lightning put an end to the third Sun, Four-Rain, with a rain of fire. The fourth Sun, Four-Water, ended in a massive flood that lasted for 52 years. The fifth and present Sun, Four-Earthquake, was created by the rain god and is doomed to be destroyed by a tremendous earthquake.

The Aztecs believed that their mission was to prevent the fifth destruction of the Earth, and that the only way of doing this was to give offerings and make sacrifices.

FOLK BELIEFS

Belief in the power of witchcraft and the devil is widespread, and good and evil spirits are prominent figures in folktales. *Brujería* (brew-hay-REE-ya), or witchcraft, is really a form of Indian medicine practiced in some rural areas. The *curandero* (cur-ahn-DE-roh), or witch doctor, is believed to have special healing powers and uses herbs and other traditional medicines to treat illnesses that do not respond to conventional Western medicine. For example, people from the city travel to Indian villages to ask a *curandero* for special powders and rituals that they hope will improve their love life.

A traditional remedy for a sick baby involves the *curandero* rubbing garlic paste on the baby's body, hanging a ring of garlic around the baby's neck, praying, and holding an egg up to the sun; if the *curandero* can see a small circle in the white part of the egg, it means that someone has looked at the baby with "sight that is too strong," and the treatment of garlic paste and prayer is continued.

An Indian medicine display offers traditional herbal remedies for a variety of illnesses.

LANGUAGE

WHILE INDIAN LANGUAGES have continued to flourish in some Central and South American countries—Mayan in Guatemala, Quechua in Peru, and Guaraní in Paraguay, for example—the indigenous languages of El Salvador have died out in daily use. Nahua and Lenca, derived from the Nahuatl language of the Aztecs, began to decline when Spain colonized El Salvador in the 16th century and most Indians became assimilated into Spanish-American culture. The massacre of 30,000 Indians in 1932 further eroded the use of indigenous languages—it was a turning point in Salvadoran history when most of the country's remaining Indians were forced to abandon their native languages, customs, and costumes in order to survive. Spanish is now the official language of El Salvador and is spoken by the vast majority of its citizens.

Left: **Spanish dominates almost every aspect of Salvadoran life, and all shop and street signs are in Spanish.**

Opposite: **A mural depicts Facundo Guardado, the 1999 presidential candidate for the FMLN party.**

The phenomenon of military rule in El Salvador and throughout Latin America has spawned such words as junta and generalissimo, which are understood everywhere.

INDIGENOUS LANGUAGES

Pipil, a Nahua language, and Chilanga, a Lenca language, are almost extinct in El Salvador, spoken by fewer than 2,000 Indians. The most obvious legacy of these languages exists in the country's geographical names. Cuscatlán, the Nahua name for the area that includes present-day El Salvador, means Land of the Jewel. Towns and villages such as Chalchuapa, Nahuizalco, and Zacatecoluca all bear names of Pipil origin. Many of the natural landmarks also retain their indigenous names, such as the Izalco Volcano, the Lempa River, and Lake Coatepeque. Most of the volcanoes have both an Indian name and a Spanish name: the San Salvador Volcano, for instance, is also known as Quetzaltepec, meaning mountain of quetzal birds in Nahua.

SPANISH

The Spanish spoken in El Salvador and other Central and South American countries is close to that of Spain, although there are some variations in local vocabulary and expressions. A soft drink, for example, is called a *gaseosa* (ga-say-OH-sah) in El Salvador and Honduras, a soda (SOH-dah) in Panama, and a *fresco* (FRAY-skoh) in Nicaragua. One feature common to the pronunciation in all of Spanish America is the tendency to make *s*, *z*, and soft *c* into the same sound *s*.

Although Spanish has replaced the indigenous languages in El Salvador, it has also been influenced by them. When the colonists came across new types of food and animals, they used an approximation of the native Indian names to create new words: thus *maíz* (may-EES, corn), *cacao* (ka-KAH-oh, cocoa), and *ananás* (ah-nah-NAHS, pineapple), as well as tapir, jaguar, and llama.

SPANISH: LANGUAGE OF THE CONQUISTADORES

In the 10th century, at the height of the Arabic civilization, the survival of Spanish in the world seemed unlikely. A few hundred years later, however, Spanish had become a major colonizing language, and today, Spanish is spoken by 12 times as many people outside than inside Spain.

Spanish gained its first foothold in the Americas when the explorer Hernán Cortés landed in 1519 and overthrew Montezuma's Aztec Empire *(below)*. As the Spanish conquistadores spread across the continent in search of gold, they brought their language with them.

Spanish is now the official language of all mainland countries in Central and South America, with the exception of Brazil, Belize, and the Guyanas. From Mexico to the tip of Argentina, Spanish is spoken by more than 300 million people.

Salvadoran Spanish includes animal references. For example, when Salvadorans sit down after a long day and sigh, "Me duelan mis patas," they are voicing the equivalent of "My dogs (feet) are killing me." Patas literally means paws. Salvadorans also refer to their children as patojos, *which is a derivative of* pato, *or duck.*

SALVADORAN PRONUNCIATION

Unlike Spanish speakers in some Latin American countries, Salvadorans typically speak clearly and precisely, pronouncing every syllable of every word. Here are some examples:

a	*a* as in *cart*
e	*e* as in *they* or *a* as in *day*
i	*ee* as in *meet*
o	*o* as in *note*
u	*oo* as in *toot* or *u* as in *flute*
y	*ee* as in *meet* or *y* as in *yet*
b	*b* as in *boy*
c	*s* as in *sit* when before *e* or *i*, or *k* as in *kind*
ch	*ch* as in *child*
d	*d* as in *dog*; or resembles *th* as in *they* when at the end of a word
f	*f* as in *off*
g	*g* as in *go*, or, when before *e* or *i*, a guttural *ch* as in *loch*
h	silent
j	*h* as in *hat*
l	*l* as in *ball*
ll	*y* as in *yet*
m	*m* as in *map*
n	*n* as in *noon*
ñ	*ny* as in *canyon*
p	*p* as in *purse*
q	*k* as in *kind*
r	rolled, especially when at the beginning of a word
rr	strongly rolled
s	*s* as in *sit*
t	*t* as in *tilt*
v	*b* as in *boy*
x	*x* as in *exit*
z	*s* as in *sit*

NAMES AND TITLES

Many Salvadorans follow the Spanish custom of having two or more surnames, taking the patrimonial surname from both parents to form the surname. For instance, Liliana Guadalupe Escobar Hernández officially has four names: the first two are hers alone; the third name, Escobar, is her father's surname, which was also his father's family name; the fourth name, Hernández, is her mother's family name. Formally, Liliana is known as Señorita Escobar Hernández, often shortened to Señorita Escobar. If she marries a man named Oscar Hurtado Gómez, she will take the patrilineal part of his surname and add it to hers: Liliana Guadalupe Escobar Hurtado. Then she will formally be called Señora Hurtado.

NONVERBAL COMMUNICATION

Nonverbal forms of communication provide important clues to a country's culture and people. As in most Hispanic cultures, Salvadorans greet each other and say goodbye with a single kiss on the cheek. Between men and women, and among women, a single meeting is enough of a basis to salute each other with a kiss. Men exchange handshakes with their male acquaintances and hugs with close male friends.

THE MEDIA

The clandestine radio station Radio Venceremos played a crucial role during the war, providing guerrillas and civilians with news of the war and details of the army's activities. The FMLN operated the station from a cave in the Morazán Mountains. Today the main radio stations in El Salvador are located in the capital city. There are four commercial television stations. Rebuilding the communication infrastructure was a post-war priority. As a result, most of the major Salvadoran cities have Internet facilities, with more than 4,000 hosts and 550,000 users.

Radio plays an important role in providing news to adult Salvadorans.

NEWSPAPERS

Salvadorans have a variety of newspapers to choose from. *La Prensa Gráfica*, *El Diario de Hoy*, and *La Noticia* are published every morning, while *El Diario El Mundo* and *Diario Latino* appear in the afternoon. In 2004 the dailies had a total circulation of 281,000.

As in many Latin American countries where the press is subjected to censorship, most papers tell the news from the government's point of view. Although *La Prensa Gráfica* is said to provide the best coverage of day-to-day news events, *Diario Latino* has the reputation of being the most objective in its coverage of news.

The Internet has provided another option for news reporting. Four out of the five dailies provide news on the Internet to compliment their newspapers. In addition, *El Faro*, *Raíces*, *San Salvador News*, and *Terra* offer dedicated Internet-based news Websites.

ARTS

EL SALVADOR'S MOST NOTABLE developments in the areas of literature, music, and painting have occurred in the last 200 years. It was only after independence that national art institutions were established, including the first music conservatory, symphony orchestra, and academy of art.

Given El Salvador's turbulent past, it is not surprising that much of the country's artistic expression has been influenced by politics. Paintings, plays, books, and music typically contain elements that are political in nature. At least three of the best-known Salvadoran writers have been forced to flee government repression for their political activities, and they live in exile abroad.

El Salvador also has a strong tradition of popular art in the form of folk music, popular theater, and folk art. Elements of indigenous art have begun to influence Salvadoran music and painting.

Left: **This mural shows a typical Salvadoran scene of a family working on a coffee plantation.**

Opposite: **A Salvadoran woman sells figurines of deer made of rattan. Since the time of the Maya, crafts have played a prominent role among the Indians of Central America.**

ANCIENT ARTS AND CRAFTS

The life-size statue of an ancient priest is displayed at the national museum.

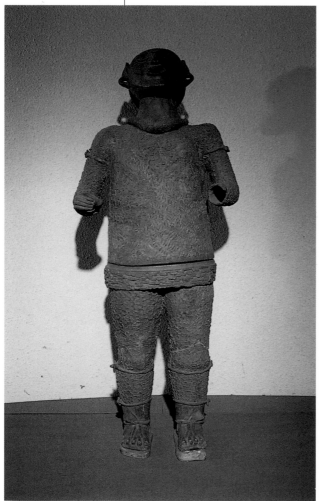

Most of what is known of Mayan and Aztec art forms is drawn from archaeological discoveries of ancient artifacts. Musical instruments, pottery vessels, stone sculptures, and jewelry made from copper, gold, and jade attest to the magnificence of the crafts produced by Indians thousands of years ago. Many of the artifacts unearthed during archaeological expeditions at the ruins of ancient cities in El Salvador are now housed in the Museo Nacional Davíd J. Guzmán—the national museum in San Salvador—and at the Tazumal Museum.

Musical instruments include pipes with as many as six finger holes; drums, called *huehuetls* (hway-HWAY-tls), made from wood or clay and originally covered with deerskin; marimbas, or wooden xylophones, which were introduced to the Pipil Indians from Mexico and Guatemala; the *pito* (PEE-toh), a high-pitched whistle that sounds like a flute; and the *chirmía* (cheer-MEE-ah), which is a pipe with a reed mouthpiece that sounds rather like a clarinet. Percussion instruments include the *tambor* (tam-BOHR), a large drum played with one hand on each side, and the *tun* (TOON), a small box drum.

PAINTING

It was not until the 20th century that El Salvador produced notable painters. The most famous contemporary Salvadoran painter is José Mejía Vides, who is sometimes called the "Painter of Panchimalco" because he often portrays small-town life in his paintings. His vivid, simple style shows the influence of Mexico's famous muralists and of the French painter Paul Gauguin.

Julia Díaz is El Salvador's best-known female painter. She studied in Paris, and her work has been exhibited in the United States, Europe, and Latin America.

Other contemporary Salvadoran painters include Raúl Elas Reyes, Luis Ángel Salinas, Camilio Minero, and Noé Canjura, all of whom have shown their work internationally.

A notable and unique school of art has been founded by Salvadoran painter Fernando Llort in La Palma, a town in the mountains north of San Salvador. La Palma art uses bright colors and a naive style to portray religious themes, as well as the peasants, the farm animals, and the red-roofed white adobe houses of rural El Salvador. The images are painted onto various items, such as wooden crosses, towels, or chests of drawers, cast into ceramics, or finely etched on seeds to be worn as pendants. Fernando Llort has also produced many excellent sculptures and canvas paintings, which he displays in his own gallery, El Árbol de Dios, in San Salvador.

Shopkeepers use art to attract customers and advertise their wares.

Right: **A craftsman in Ilobasco paints ceramic figures.**

Below: **Hammocks and other colorfully woven textiles have been hand-made in the village of San Sebastián for well over a hundred years.**

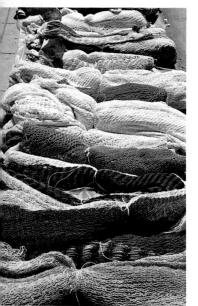

HANDICRAFTS

Since the time of the Maya many thousands of years ago, crafts have played a prominent role among the Indians of Central America. Musical instruments, pottery vessels, stone sculptures, architectural ornaments, and jewelry found at the sites of ruined cities offer proof of the level of skill attained by Mayan craftsmen. In some areas, entire communities specialized in a particular craft. Craftsmen were organized into guilds and enjoyed considerable prestige in society.

Several Indian villages near San Salvador continue to specialize in traditional handicrafts. Ilobasco, one of the country's foremost traditional craft villages, is famous for its intricate ceramics and *sorpresas* (sorh-PRAY-sas), or surprises, which are tiny clay figures and nativity scenes hidden inside walnut-sized oval shells.

Basketry is the specialty of Nahuizalco, a Pipil Indian village. Colorful hammocks and other woven textiles made on handmade wooden looms form the basis of San Sebastián's economy.

LITERATURE

Poetry has a strong tradition in El Salvador and is extremely popular among people from all walks of life. The 19th century poet Juan José Cañas Gavidia spent most of his life living abroad and writing nostalgically about El Salvador's lakes and volcanoes.

Poet, essayist, playwright, translator, historian, and dramatist Francisco Antonio Gavidia died in 1955 at the age of 92. His most important poem, *To Central America*, condemned tyranny and expressed faith in democracy and the unity of Central America.

Salvador Salazar Arrué, who wrote under the pen name Salarrué, was a novelist, short story writer, and painter. His short story, *Cuentos de Barro*, or *Tales of Mud*, is said to mark the beginning of the modern Central American short story genre.

Two of the best and most controversial writers of the 20th century are Roque Dalton and Manlio Argueta. Dalton was a poet and historian who was born into a wealthy family but spoke out against El Salvador's social injustices. He was arrested by government forces and sentenced to be executed, but he escaped and went into exile from 1960 to 1973. When he returned to El Salvador, he joined the guerrilla army but was charged with spying. He was tried and executed by the guerrillas in 1975. *Clandestine Poems*, the collection of poetry that he wrote when he returned secretly to El Salvador for a short while in 1965, was translated into English in 1984.

Argueta writes about the daily life and struggles of the Salvadoran peasants. He was expelled from El Salvador because of his political activism and lived in exile in Costa Rica until the end of the civil war in El Salvador. His books, *One Day of Life* and *Cuzcatlán*, have been translated into English.

A tribute to Roque Dalton, a prominent Salvadoran writer who was exiled by government forces in 1960 and executed by the guerrilla army in 1975.

Folk musicians play at a festival in a village of Santa Cruz Melada.

MUSIC

Formal music performances are held at San Salvador's National Theater. David Granadino and Felipe Soto are two renowned 19th century composers whose music is still performed today. One of El Salvador's most famous 20th century composers is María Mendoza de Baratta, who is greatly influenced by indigenous Salvadoran music.

Canción popular (kan-see-OHN poh-poo-LAHR), or folk music, which describes daily life and current events in El Salvador, is performed in bars, cafés, at music festivals, and at an open forum called a *peña* (PAY-nya), where anyone from the audience can stand up and play or sing. Andean folk music, the distinctive Incan music of the Andes played on pan pipes and flutes, is also popular in El Salvador.

THEATER

Formal theatrical performances are held at the ornate National Theater in San Salvador. Contemporary dramatists include Waldo Chávez Velasco, who writes fantasy, and Italo López Vallecillos and Alvaro Menén Desleal, both distinguished popular authors of political and philosophical works.

Popular theater, on the other hand, is usually performed in cafés and at outdoor festivals, and often draws from political subject matter. During the civil war, this type of theater was often performed with a certain degree of risk, because it usually carried a message of protest against the government, and the military often responded with harassment and violence against the performers.

POLITICAL ART

Political murals and graffiti adorn many university campus buildings, banners, and walls throughout the city of San Salvador. Salvadorans have used this popular art form to express their feelings and frustrations about various aspects of the civil war. The Mothers of the Disappeared mounted photographs and paintings of their loved ones onto banners  when staging their demonstrations. Students sprayed anti-U.S. slogans and drawings of Uncle Sam and American troops onto walls, and leftwing supporters wrote protests against government violence in huge letters on the city's sidewalks.

LEISURE

DAILY LIFE IS HARD WORK in El Salvador, especially in rural areas. With the whole family toiling long hours just to get by, there is little time left for play and little or no money for toys or hobbies. Salvadoran children still play when they can, of course, making toys from sticks, tin cans, stones, or rags, and playing *mica* (MEE-ka), or tag. Soccer is extremely popular, and those who cannot afford to buy a proper soccer ball make do with a nylon stocking wrapped around a ball of rags. After the evening meal, friends and neighbors often gather together. Wealthier Salvadorans living in the capital have more sophisticated leisure choices: they can dine in fine restaurants, see plays at the National Theater, dance in nightclubs, or listen to concerts performed by El Salvador's symphony orchestra.

Left: **Taking a break from the heat with watermelon provides a sweet and refreshing afternoon treat.**

Opposite: **Mountain-biking in a park in Morazán.**

SPORTS

Volleyball, basketball, baseball, and softball are popular in El Salvador, but soccer is the country's national sport. Its fans are passionate in their enjoyment of the game, whether they are playing it themselves or just watching it. Almost every city has a soccer stadium, and young boys join neighborhood or school teams at an early age, hoping to be chosen one day to play for the Selección Nacional, the national team.

SOCCER WAR Unfortunately, politics can intrude into the realm of sports, as it did in the Soccer War of 1969. At the time, approximately 300,000 Salvadorans were living illegally in Honduras, refugees from the poverty and repression in overcrowded El Salvador. Resentment among Hondurans against the Salvadoran squatters had been growing, and

Salvadorans love soccer, whether they are playing it, supporting a local game, or watching their national team on television.

hostilities rose to a fevered pitch in a soccer game played between the
two countries as a World Cup preliminary in June 1969 in San Salvador.
Salvadoran fans harassed Honduran team members and fans and insulted
the Honduran flag and national anthem. Salvadorans still in Honduras
suffered from retaliatory acts by Hondurans. El Salvador launched a
military strike against Honduras and, although the war was brief, more
than 2,000 lives were lost.

WATER SPORTS   Popular in El Salvador, especially during the hottest
months, are water sports. Wealthier Salvadorans enjoy swimming at
private clubs or beaches, water-skiing, boating, and fishing, while poor
rural children are happy simply to splash about in lakes or rivers while
their mothers wash clothes. One of the most popular spots for swimming
is Los Chorros, a beautiful park near San Salvador.

A family gathers around to listen to the radio.

TELEVISION AND RADIO

In a small town on a Saturday night, it is not uncommon to see half the townspeople crowded around the doorway of a single small house lit by the bluish glow of a television—especially if a soccer match is on. Although El Salvador has several television stations, television sets are scarce, due to the widespread poverty and shortage of electricity. There are only about 200 television sets for every 1,000 people, and in rural areas television is almost non-existent. Those who do have a set sometimes offset the cost by charging their neighbors a few cents to watch it. Radios are more prevalent, and El Salvador has over 60 radio stations. Unlike its larger neighbors, El Salvador does not produce any of its own movies or television programs; most of them are imported from the United States or Mexico and are either dubbed into Spanish or given Spanish subtitles. Only city dwellers have access to movie theaters.

STORYTELLING

A more common form of entertainment is storytelling. It does not cost anything, does not require any electrical gadgets or a knowledge of reading, and it can be used by mothers to entertain their children while carrying out household tasks. The same stories are heard all over the country, although they often have regional variations; common themes include the devil, who is typically disguised, and the struggle between good and evil. Among Indians, ancient legends about the creation of the world and of human beings are an important part of the culture, as well as a form of entertainment.

Folktales and legends are passed down through the generations by word of mouth.

DEVILISH FOLKTALES

The devil is a central figure in Salvadoran folktales. People try to avoid him out of fear that he will tempt them into giving their souls to him. One well-known story is *Justo Juez de la Noche*, or *Just Judge of the Night*. The Just Judge is a tall man wearing a black suit who appears only at midnight. No one has ever seen his face, but his eyes are "like fire." He usually appears before lone travelers, especially in rural areas.

In one version of the story, a man named Julio is walking alone one night when he sees a very tall man blocking his path. The tall man, of course, is the Just Judge, although Julio does not know it. They walk and talk together for a long time. Suddenly, the Just Judge whips out his machete and tries to strike Julio with it, but Julio is experienced with a machete. He manages to strike the Just Judge with his own machete, but the blow has no effect. Instead, the Just Judge simply laughs with a roar so loud that it can be heard from miles away. Julio sees the red eyes for the first time, and he runs away to avoid losing his soul, but he cannot escape losing his mind.

THE TOWN SQUARE

Small towns and villages in El Salvador, as in much of Latin America, are built around a central square, or plaza, which serves as the hub of the town's social, economic, and political life. The most important buildings, such as the church, the town hall, and the main stores border the plaza. The square is usually planted with trees, flowers, and shrubs, and is a popular center for playing games, relaxing, and socializing.

MUSIC AND DANCING

Salvadorans love getting together to sing, play music, and dance. The songs are often religious in nature, especially in church communities, or they tell a story. Rock music from abroad is popular among young people and is played in nightclubs and discos in San Salvador, but everyone enjoys dancing to Latino music, such as the lively *cumbia* (coom-BEE-ah) and salsa or the romantic *ranchera* (rahn-CHEH-ra).

THE AMERICAN INFLUENCE

American television programs, food brands, fashion trends, and leisure activities have made their presence felt throughout much of the world, and El Salvador is no exception.

Baseball and skateboarding are popular pastimes. Fast-food restaurants, such as McDonald's, Pizza Hut, and Dunkin' Donuts, are easily found in the capital city of San Salvador and are much frequented by the young.

Coca-Cola and Pepsi are the best-known brands of soft drinks, and blue jeans are worn by men and women in El Salvador from all walks of life.

American situation comedies and series dominate the country's television channels, providing young Salvadorans with examples of the latest hairstyles, clothing, and verbal expressions.

Pop songs from popular American music bands can be heard on many of El Salvador's radio stations.

FESTIVALS

THE INFLUENCE OF El Salvador's long Roman Catholic tradition combined with its Indian heritage have created a lively and colorful festival culture. The people of El Salvador celebrate several holidays as a nation, observed primarily in smaller groups through their towns and churches.

Most of the major festivals and holidays are religious and are the cause of particularly lengthy revelry—Christmas and Easter celebrations each last a full week. In addition, each city, village, and town has an annual festival for its patron saint, and some small towns embellish their town festivals with rich indigenous traditions.

Opposite: **Salvadoran youths paint their faces to participate in celebrations for Bolas de Fuego, or Balls of Fire. The festival follows a cultural tradition going back 300 years to recreate the plight of Saint Jeronimo, who was pelted by balls of fire from Satan as he prayed in the mountains.**

HOLIDAYS AND FESTIVALS

New Year's Eve	December 31
New Year's Day	January 1
Palm Sunday	March/April (variable)
Easter Sunday	March/April (variable)
Labor Day	May 1
Day of the Virgin of Fátima	May 13
Festival of El Salvador del Mundo	August 3–6
Independence Day	September 15
Columbus Day	October 12
All Souls' Day	November 2
Anniversary of First Call for Independence	November 5
Day of the Virgin of Guadalupe	December 12
Christmas	December 25–31

SEMANA SANTA

Holy Week, or Semana Santa, begins the week before Easter with Palm Sunday and is cause for grand celebrations within the Catholic Church. Catholics celebrate Palm Sunday, the day representing Jesus' entry into Jerusalem, by walking to Mass bearing flowers and palm branches. In some towns the streets are carpeted with flowers and lined with pictures of the Virgin Mary and Jesus.

All the stages of Christ's crucifixion and ascent into heaven are played out through dramatic ritual and elaborate celebration. The Last Supper is observed at Mass when the priest washes the feet of 12 men, just as the Bible says that Jesus washed the feet of his 12 disciples. On the Thursday, Friday, or Saturday of Semana Santa, they symbolically mourn the death of Jesus by giving up some personal comfort or luxury.

During Semana Santa, international surfing competitions are held at Zunzal, one of the best surfing beaches in Central America.

Semana Santa

On Good Friday, a group of people carry a cross and a life-size image of Jesus through town, while singing songs of his suffering. When the procession arrives at the church, it is met by more people carrying an image of Jesus nailed to the cross. In the town of Izalco, the image of Jesus on the cross is so large that it takes 75 people to carry it. The image of Jesus is taken down from the cross at three o'clock in the afternoon. People wrap the image in white sheets and keep a candlelight vigil at the church throughout the night.

The tone of the entire day is very serious. Children are not supposed to run, because Judas ran after he betrayed Christ. Indeed, children generally do not play on Good Friday, nor do people travel, out of respect for Jesus' torturous journey to Calvary. Semana Santa is sincerely celebrated in El Salvador because so many people feel that it is symbolic of their own suffering and their hope for renewed life.

On Easter Saturday, people spend the day relaxing. They might sleep in late, then pack a lunch of tamales, watermelon, tortillas, and beans before spending the afternoon at the ocean or the nearest river. In the evening, they attend Mass. Outside the church, they circle around a bonfire; the priest uses the flames to light a candle, which in turn is used to light all the parishioners' candles. Then they enter the church in a lighted procession, which is meant to symbolize Christ before his resurrection from the dead.

The somber tone of Semana Santa ends on Easter Sunday, which is known as Pascua. People joyously celebrate by marching in a procession, again carrying the image of Jesus. They receive a blessing from the priest with holy water, and some people bring their animals to be blessed as well.

Semana Santa is especially beautiful in the smaller towns, where people celebrate the holiday to the fullest.

The Easter season begins on Ash Wednesday, the first day of Lent. Lent is observed for 40 days before Easter Sunday. During this time, people remember the sacrifice of Jesus through fasting and penitence.

CHRISTMAS

Townspeople honor their patron saint by carrying an image of the saint through the streets during the festival procession.

The season of Christmas begins a full month before Christmas Day, and continues into January. As with Semana Santa, it is especially celebrated in the Catholic Church. Beginning on November 26, church members practice *posadas* (po-SAH-das), or inns, taking statues of the Virgin Mary and Joseph from house to house every night until December 23, and spending a few hours singing, eating, and praying together at each house.

The holiday season reaches its climax on the night of December 24, which is called La Noche Buena, or The Good Night. Everyone attends midnight Mass and then gathers at home to celebrate, often all night long. They drink and dance, open presents, and eat specially prepared foods such as tamales and turkey. Salvadoran children receive their gifts from El Niño Dios, or Baby Jesus, on Christmas Eve.

People who can afford Christmas ornaments usually decorate lavishly. They often have a Christmas tree, but more common is the nativity scene, or *nacimiento* (na-see-mee-EN-toh), with statues or figurines that are often life-size. *Nacimientos* can be very elaborate, with farms and villages and little roads leading to the manger. People with fewer resources decorate a single small branch or dry bush to create their Christmas tree. Decorations are not taken down until January 6, the Day of the Three Kings, or Epiphany, which commemorates the day that the Three Kings finally arrived to see the baby Jesus after following the Star of Bethlehem.

New Year's Eve, December 31, is another occasion for festive eating, drinking, and dancing. Dinner typically consists of tamales and a roasted hen. However, it can also be a rather melancholy holiday, filled with hugging and crying as people ask pardon of their loved ones for the sins of the past year and promise to behave better in the coming year.

PATRON SAINTS' FESTIVALS

Because the Catholic Church has such a strong tradition in El Salvador, every city in the country has a patron saint, celebrated with a festival sometime during the year. The festivals usually last for an entire week and include a parade, soccer tournaments, and lots of eating, drinking, and dancing in the streets. The festivals are particularly colorful in Indian towns and villages; the celebrants dress up in their native costumes, with vivid plumage and colorful dress that is unique to their indigenous group. Their parade includes traditional indigenous dances and music. The biggest festival is held on August 6 for El Salvador del Mundo, or The Holy Savior of the World, patron saint of the whole country.

FOOD

THE STAPLE DIET of most Salvadorans, especially in rural areas, is beans, rice, and tortillas, mainly because they cannot afford much more. Despite the high starch content of these staple foods, most Salvadorans only get about two-thirds of the calories they need, and malnutrition is one of the leading causes of death among the rural population. Meat, poultry, and fish are a rare treat. The choice of food available to wealthier city dwellers is much wider, and includes a variety of vegetables, fruit, poultry, and seafood. San Salvador is well known for its Chinese, French, and Italian restaurants, and for the abundance of excellent seafood; shrimp, lobster, and swordfish are all caught daily off El Salvador's coast. *Pupusas* (poo-POO-sas), the national fast food of filled tortillas, are sold at food stalls, markets, and small restaurants throughout El Salvador.

Left: **Live chickens ready for market in Santa Rosa.**

Opposite: **A Salvadoran woman makes and sells tortillas at her street stall.**

121

THE TYPICAL SALVADORAN DIET

A Salvadoran worker prepares to eat a typical lunch, which consists of tortillas and beans.

In rural areas, people eat breakfast before the sun comes up, so the men can start working in the fields very early. Breakfast, or *desayuno* (de-sah-YOO-no), is a simple affair, consisting of coffee and a hot tortilla, which is sometimes diced and soaked in warm milk. Lunch, called *almuerzo* (al-mu-AIR-so), is the largest meal of the day. It typically consists of soup, with tortillas, rice, corn, or beans, and very occasionally meat, fish, or poultry. As in most Latin American countries, lunch usually lasts for about two hours, giving field workers a chance to rest before resuming work until dark. Dinner, or the *cena* (SAY-nah), is often a lighter meal, consisting of vegetables, tortillas, and beans.

For urban Salvadorans, breakfast usually consists of coffee, bread, and fruit. The midday meal is often tortillas with rice and beans and is not necessarily the largest meal of the day. Urban Salvadorans are not typically able to take a siesta in the middle of the day, unlike many other Latin Americans, although some shops do close for an hour or two at lunchtime. Families usually eat the evening meal together, which may include soup or vegetables, beans, rice, tortillas, and fish or meat. City supermarkets also provide a variety of processed foods imported from abroad.

The Salvadoran government has set 2,200 calories per person per day as the national standard for caloric intake. However, most Salvadorans get far less than the national average because they do not have the means to buy or produce adequate food. The lack of protein leads to serious nutritional problems, especially among children and pregnant women in

TORTILLA-MAKING

Making tortillas is considered to be the exclusive task of women. A woman starts making the day's supply of tortillas for her family early in the morning. The traditional method of making tortillas from scratch and by hand is still used by the typical rural woman.

First she must soak or boil the hard kernels of ripe corn in a mixture of water and white lime, which turns the corn into a starchy dough. She uses a handstone called a *mano* (MAH-no) to grind the dough on a grinding stone, called a *metate* (may-TAH-tay). Then she kneads the dough by hand, slapping it back and forth between her hands until it forms a thin, round patty. When the tortillas are ready to be cooked, she fries them on a hot griddle, called a *comal* (co-MAHL).

rural parts of the country. Economic factors, for example plunging coffee prices, also affect Salvadorans' ability to buy food for themselves and their families. The Ministry of Health reported that malnutrition increased from 7 percent in 1998 to 85 percent in 2002 in the Juayua municipality.

DRINKS

Although coffee is El Salvador's primary export, the coffee served in El Salvador is often instant. Whether it is instant or brewed, it tends to be

weak and bland. Salvadorans often dilute it with barley juice, and in rural areas, the taste is further altered by the necessity of adding bleach to the water to help prevent cholera. The most common cold drinks are *gaseosas* (ga-say-OH-sas), or sodas, and *refrescos* (ray-fres-KOS), which are fruit juices mixed with sugar and water. Locally brewed beer and spirits are also popular. Tic-Tack, a particularly strong spirit made from sugarcane, has been nicknamed the national liquor of El Salvador. Like vodka, it is colorless, but has an even higher alcohol content.

Above: **Bottles of Tic-Tack, the national liquor, stand on a supermarket shelf.**

Right: **In rural El Salvador, coffee is ground by hand.**

IN THE KITCHEN

Kitchens in rural houses are usually located outside the house, either in a separate building or under a roof extending from the house. The women cook over a fire, or on a raised cement platform oven with a hollow center for the fire, over which they put a grill or griddle made of clay or metal. They must walk to a river or stream to fetch water, which they ration carefully throughout the day for their cooking and cleaning purposes.

Middle- and upper-class families, on the other hand, usually have at least one maid to help with cooking and cleaning. The maid will often do the shopping, although the *señora* (se-NYO-rah), or lady of the house, will usually prepare the list for her, and may even accompany her to the market. The *señora* also directs the daily menu, but the maid does most of the cooking. The kitchens in these houses are modern compared to rural kitchens, but they typically lack appliances such as dishwashers and washing machines because the maid cleans the dishes and often washes the clothes by hand.

Rural kitchens in El Salvador are very basic. Most do not have electricity or running water.

A typical grocery store in a small town offers a limited range of goods, and the food is not refrigerated.

MARKETS

The traditional open-air market in El Salvador is crowded with close-set stalls offering a wide variety of goods: hot tortillas and tamales, handmade baskets, colorful flowers, fresh fruit and vegetables, live chickens or pigs, shoes, clothes, hammocks, and dishes. The air is full of rich aromas and noisy bargaining by women carrying netted handbags or large wicker baskets on their heads to hold their daily purchases. Shoppers thread their way through row upon row of fresh produce, including bananas, mangoes, melons, carrots, corn, avocadoes, cabbages, tomatoes, peppers, garlic, and potatoes. In the larger cities, modern supermarkets have supplanted some of the open-air markets, providing shoppers with an array of refrigerated, processed, and canned foods.

A modern supermarket in San Salvador.

SALVADORAN SPECIALTIES

One of the most delicious and interesting foods is the *pupusa*, which is unique to El Salvador. *Pupusas* are small, thick corn tortillas filled with sausage, cheese, or beans and served hot, with salad or salsa. They are sold in *pupuserías* (poo-poo-say-REE-ah) all over El Salvador.

Tamales—steamed rolls of cornmeal stuffed with shredded meat, peppers, and corn and wrapped in corn husks—are another popular food, common to many Central American countries. Tamales take a great deal of time to prepare and are considered a dish for special occasions.

A favorite soup in El Salvador is *sopa de pata* (SOH-pah deh PAH-tah), or hoof soup, made from the hoof of a cow or an ox, with vegetables and sometimes beef tripe. *Sopa de pata* is made year-round, but it is especially popular during holidays and at family gatherings.

It takes an experienced hand to make *pupusas*, a Salvadoran specialty of stuffed tortillas.

FOOD: FAST, FROZEN

The number of families in El Salvador's cities with two or more working members is increasing, and longer hours spent at work translate into less time to prepare home-made meals.

The convenience of processed frozen food is quickly attracting the attention of busy urban Salvadorans. Apart from fast-food restaurants, processed frozen food is gaining popularity in Salvadorans' kitchens and is mostly imported from the United States. Urban Salvadorans are getting acquainted with meat patties, frozen pizzas, precooked vegetables, ice creams, concentrated juices, and canned stews. French fries and canned sodas are particularly well-liked. An array of fast food restaurants is sprouting in the cities, and fries and sodas are fast catching up with traditional favorites, such as *pupusas* and *refrescos*.

The idea of freezing prepared food is fast catching on among enterprising Salvadorans. For years, Salvadorans in the United States enjoyed their national food at *pupuserías*. Today they have the option of stocking up on *pupusas* imported from El Salvador; these *pupusas* look like packed, precooked frozen pizzas. *Pupusas* may well make their way into ovens in the United States, and in El Salvador they may well be stored alongside the popular French fries in freezers.

PUPUSAS

This recipe makes 12 cheese *pupusas*.

3 cups *masa harina* (cornmeal, found in grocery stores)
2 teaspoons salt
1$^1/_2$ cups warm water
$^1/_2$ lb (227 g) Monterrey Jack cheese, grated
$^1/_4$ green bell pepper, minced
vegetable oil for frying

In a large bowl, combine *masa harina* with salt and water. Mix until it becomes a pliable dough. Cover with plastic wrap and refrigerate for one hour. Mix cheese with green pepper. Set aside. Prepare the *cortido*. Set aside.

Remove dough from the refrigerator. Divide into six balls, then divide each ball again into four balls. Place a piece of plastic wrap on a flat surface. Place one ball of dough on top of the plastic and cover with a second piece of plastic. Use a rolling pin to flatten it into a circle about 3 inches (7.6 cm) in diameter. Do the same with the remaining balls of dough.

Remove the plastic wrap from the dough and place about two teaspoons of the cheese mixture in the center of the circle, leaving a $^1/_4$-inch (0.6-cm) border. Cover with a second circle of dough and seal by pressing the edges together. Repeat with remaining balls of dough.

Heat a thin layer of vegetable oil in a large skillet and cook a few *pupusas* at a time over moderate heat for 2 to 3 minutes per side, or until they are golden brown. Drain on paper towels and place in a warm oven while cooking the remaining *pupusas*. Serve immediately with *cortido*.

CORTIDO

1 medium onion, thinly sliced
1¹⁄₂ cups shredded green cabbage
1 large carrot, peeled and shredded
3 cloves garlic, minced
¹⁄₄ cup apple cider vinegar
2 teaspoons dried oregano
Salt and pepper to taste

Combine salad ingredients in a bowl and mix well. Season with salt and pepper and let stand for 30 minutes at room temperature before serving.

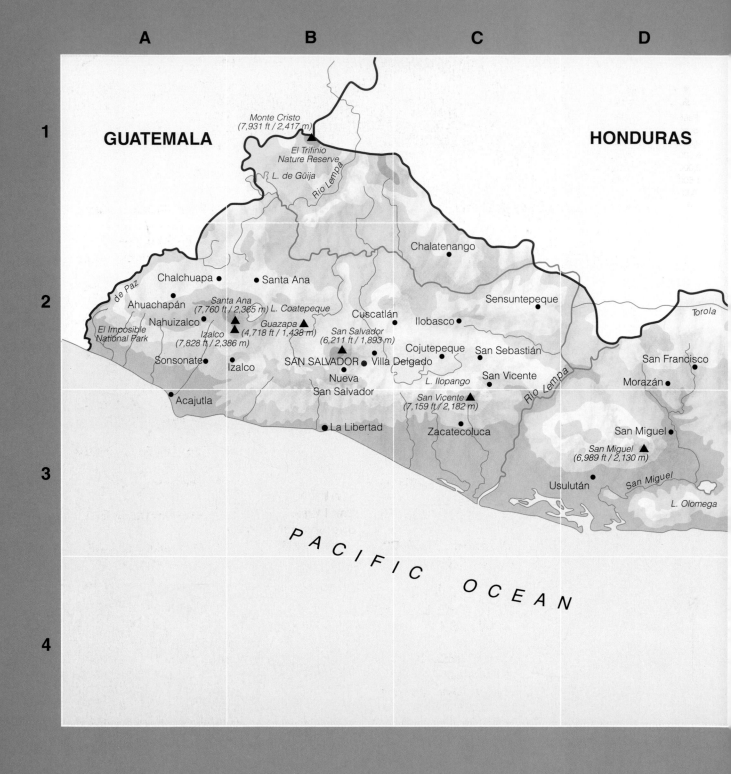

GUATEMALA

HONDURAS

Monte Cristo
(7,931 ft / 2,417 m)

El Trifinio
Nature Reserve

L. de Güija

Rio Lempa

Chalatenango

de Paz

Chalchuapa

Santa Ana

Ahuachapán

Sensuntepeque

Torola

Santa Ana
(7,760 ft / 2,365 m) L. Coatepeque

Cuscatlán

El Imposible
National Park

Nahuizalco

Guazapa

Ilobasco

Izalco
(7,828 ft / 2,386 m)

Izalco

San Salvador
(6,211 ft / 1,893 m)

Guazapa
(4,718 ft / 1,438 m)

Cojutepeque

San Sebastián

San Francisco

Sonsonate

SAN SALVADOR

Villa Delgado

L. Ilopango

San Vicente

Morazán

Nueva
San Salvador

Acajutla

San Vicente
(7,159 ft / 2,182 m)

San Miguel

La Libertad

Zacatecoluca

San Miguel
(6,989 ft / 2,130 m)

Usulután

San Miguel

L. Olomega

Rio Lempa

P A C I F I C   O C E A N

MAP OF EL SALVADOR

Acajutla, A3
Ahuachapán, A2

Chalatenango, C2
Chalchuapa, A2
Cojutepeque, C2
Cuscatlán, B2, C2

de Paz, A2

El Imposible National Park, A2
El Trifinio Nature Reserve, B1

Guatemala, A1–A2, B1
Guazapa (mountain), B2
Gulf of Fonseca, E3

Honduras, B1, C1–C2, D1–D2, E1–E3

Ilobasco, C2
Izalco (mountain), B2
Izalco, B2

La Libertad, B3
La Union, E3
Lake Coatepeque, B2
Lake de Güija, B1
Lake Ilopango, B2, C2

Lake Olomega, D3

Monte Cristo (mountain), B1
Morazán, D2

Nahuizalco, A2
Nueva San Salvador, B2

Pacific Ocean, A2–A4, B3–B4, C3–C4, D3–D4, E4

Rio Lempa (river), B1–B2, C2–C3, D2

San Francisco, D2
San Miguel, D3
San Miguel (mountain), D3

San Miguel (river), D2–D3
San Salvador, B2
San Salvador (mountain), B2
San Sebastián, C2
San Vicente, C2
San Vicente (mountain), C3
Santa Ana (mountain), B2
Santa Ana, B2
Sensuntepeque, C2
Sonsonate, A2

Torola (river), D2, E2

Usulután, D3

Villa Delgado, B2

Zacatecoluca, C3

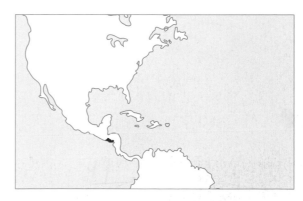

133

ECONOMIC EL SALVADOR

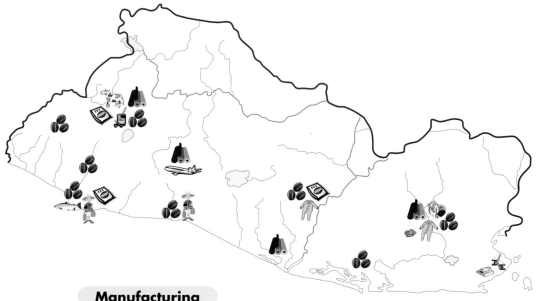

Manufacturing

 Cotton

 Dairy Products

 Food Products

 Sugar

 Textiles

 Vegetable Oil

Farming

 Cattle

 Coffee

Services

 Airport

 Tourism

Natural Resources

 Fish

 Iron

 Silver

ABOUT THE ECONOMY

GROSS DOMESTIC PRODUCT (GDP)
$31 billion

GDP PER CAPITA
$4,800 (2003)

GDP BY SECTOR
Agriculture 9.4 percent, industry 31.2 percent, services 59.3 percent (2003)

INFLATION
2.1 percent (2003)

INDUSTRIAL PRODUCTS
Processed food, beverages, petroleum, chemicals, fertilizer, textiles, furniture, light metals

AGRICULTURAL PRODUCTS
Coffee, sugar, corn, rice, beans, oilseed, cotton, sorghum, shrimp, beef, dairy products

NATURAL RESOURCES
Hydropower, geothermal power, petroleum, land

CURRENCY
Both the Salvadoran colon and U.S. dollar are legal tender in El Salvador.
1 El Salvador colon (SVC) = 100 centavos
Notes: 5, 10, 25, 50, 100, 200 colones
Coins: 1, 5, 10, 25, 50 centavos; 1 colon
US$ 1 = SVC 8.75 (April 2005)

WORKFORCE
2.6 million (2003)

WORKFORCE BY SECTOR
Agriculture 30 percent, industry 15 percent, services 55 percent (1999)

UNEMPLOYMENT RATE
6.5 percent with much underemployment (2004)

POPULATION BELOW POVERTY LINE
48 percent (1999)

EXTERNAL DEBT
$6.6 billion (2003)

PUBLIC DEBT
43.7 percent of GDP (2003)

EXPORTS
$3.2 billion (2003)

MAJOR EXPORTS
Offshore assembly exports, coffee, sugar, shrimp, textiles, chemicals, electricity

IMPORTS
$5.5 billion (2003)

MAJOR IMPORTS
Raw materials, consumer goods, capital goods, fuels, foodstuffs, petroleum, electricity

MAJOR TRADE PARTNERS
U.S., Guatemala, Honduras, Mexico

CULTURAL EL SALVADOR

El Trifinio Nature Reserve
This important conservation area is shared by three countries: El Salvador, Guatemala, and Honduras. Inside this reserve is the Monte Cristo cloud forest, one of the few remaining cloud forests in Central America.

Tazumal ruins
Located in Chalchuapa, near Santa Ana, this is the archaeological site of a 5000 B.C. Mayan settlement. Tazumal in the Mayan language means pyramid where the victims are burned. There is also a museum that displays artifacts of the Pipil, who built Tazumal.

El Imposible National Park
This park is regarded as one of the last remaining tropical rain forests in El Salvador. It is home to such animals as puma, ocelot, and harpy eagle. The park's name comes from the Impossible Pass within it, which is a steep path that olden travellers used to traverse when passing through this forest.

San Salvador
El Salvador's capital is the largest city in the country and the second-largest in Central America. It has buildings that bear Spanish architectural design and is home to the National Theater and National Palace.

Lake Coatepeque
This beautiful lake is located at the foot of the Santa Ana volcano and is a popular recreation spot.

Santa Ana volcano
Santa Ana is the highest peak in El Salvador, rising to 7,749 feet (2,362 m). Its last eruption was in 1920.

Lake Ilopango
El Salvador's largest lake fills the crater of an extinct volcano. It is located at an altitude of 1,450 feet (442 m) and has a surface area of 40 square miles (100 square km). The lake is a popular resort and tourist area.

Izalco volcano
Continuously active between 1700 until 1966, Izalco volcano was dubbed as the Lighthouse of the Pacific by seafarers in the 19th century. Molten lava running down its sides turned the volcano into a brightly glowing beacon that could be seen miles out to sea.

San Andrés ruins
This site in La Libertad was a ceremonial center of the Mayan civilization. It was inhabited by a succession of Maya, Aztec, and Pipil Indians.

Joya De Cerén ruins
The farming community at this site in La Libertad was buried by a volcanic eruption in 600 A.D., which preserves the remains in excellent condition. Artifacts and structures provide good insights into the residents' daily lives. Joya de Cerén is a UNESCO World Heritage Site.

ABOUT THE CULTURE

COUNTRY NAME
Republic of El Salvador

NATIONAL FLAG
Three equal horizontal bands of blue, white, and blue with the national coat of arms in the center of the white band; the coat of arms features a round emblem encircled by the words "Republica de El Salvador en la America Central."

NATIONAL ANTHEM
Saludemos la Patria Orgullosos (*Proudly Salute the Fatherland*). Composed by Juan Aberle and lyrics by General Juan José Cañas. Adopted as the national anthem in 1879 and officially recognized in 1953.

NATIONAL FLOWER
Izote

NATIONAL TREE
Maquilishuat

CAPITAL
San Salvador

OTHER MAJOR CITIES
Santa Ana, San Miguel

ADMINISTRATIVE DEPARTMENTS
Fourteen departments: Ahuachapan, Cabanas, Chalatenango, Cuscatlán, La Libertad, La Paz, La Unión, Morazán, San Miguel, San Salvador, Santa Ana, San Vicente, Sonsonate, Usulután

POPULATION
6,587,541 (2004)

ETHNIC GROUPS
Mestizo 90 percent, white 9 percent, Amerindian 1 percent

LIFE EXPECTANCY
Men 67.3 years, women74.7 years (2004)

LITERACY RATE
Men 82.8 percent, women 77.7 percent (2003)

OFFICIAL LANGUAGE
Spanish

MAJOR RELIGION
Roman Catholicism

IMPORTANT DATES
Easter Sunday (March/April), Day of the Virgin of Fátima (May 13), Festival of El Salvador del Mundo (August 3–6), Independence Day (15 September), Anniversary of First Call for Independence (November 5), Christmas (December 25–31)

LEADERS IN THE ARTS
Manlio Argueta (writer), Roque Dalton (writer), María Mendoza de Baratta (composer)

TIME LINE

IN EL SALVADOR	IN THE WORLD

1500 B.C.
Early Mayan civilization

753 B.C.
Rome is founded.
116–17 B.C.
The Roman Empire reaches its greatest extent, under Emperor Trajan (98–17).

A.D. 600–900
Height of Mayan civilization

A.D. 600
Height of Mayan civilization

900–1200
Mayan civilization declines.

1000
The Chinese perfect gunpowder and begin to use it in warfare.

1524
Spanish conquistador Pedro de Alvarado leads troops to attack El Salvador in search of gold and silver. Natives put up resistance.

1530
Beginning of transatlantic slave trade organized by the Portuguese in Africa.

1540
Natives overcome by disease, slavery, and weapon shortage. El Salvador becomes a Spanish colony.

1558–1603
Reign of Elizabeth I of England
1620
Pilgrims sail the *Mayflower* to America.
1776
U.S. Declaration of Independence
1789–99
The French Revolution

1821
Independence from Spain

1823
El Salvador becomes part of the United Provinces of Central America, which also includes Costa Rica, Guatemala, Honduras and Nicaragua.

1840
El Salvador becomes fully independent following the dissolution of the United Provinces of Central America.

1859–63
President Gerardo Barrios introduces coffee-growing.

1861
The U.S. Civil War begins.
1869
The Suez Canal is opened.

IN EL SALVADOR	IN THE WORLD
	1914 World War I begins.
1932 A peasant uprising led by Agustine Farabundo Marti leads to 30,000 people being killed during the suppression.	**1939** World War II begins.
	1945 The United States drops atomic bombs on Hiroshima and Nagasaki.
	1949 The North Atlantic Treaty Organization (NATO) is formed.
	1957 The Russians launch Sputnik.
1969 The Soccer War with Honduras.	**1966–69** The Chinese Cultural Revolution
1980 Archbishop Oscar Romero assassinated. Jose Napoleon Duarte becomes first civilian president since 1931.	
1983 Democracy restored with the adoption of new Constitution.	**1986** Nuclear power disaster at Chernobyl in Ukraine
	1991 Break-up of the Soviet Union
1992 Government and FMLN sign peace accord. FMLN recognized as political party.	
1993 Government declares amnesty for those implicated in human rights atrocities.	**1997** Hong Kong is returned to China.
1998 Hurricane Mitch kills 374 Salvadorans.	
2001 El Salvador adopts U.S. dollar as national currency. Earthquakes kill 1,400 people.	**2001** Terrorists crash planes in New York, Washington, D.C., and Pennsylvania.
2004 ARENA candidate Tony Saca wins presidential elections.	**2003** War in Iraq

GLOSSARY

brujería (brew-hay-REE-ya)
Witchcraft that is really a form of Indian medicine practiced in some rural areas.

choza (CHO-sah)
A rural house made of woven branches and covered with mud.

coup
The removal of a government, illegally and by force, usually by the military.

curandero (cur-ahn-DE-roh)
An Indian witch doctor or healer.

Cuscatlán
The Indian name for the region that now includes El Salvador. It means Land of the Jewel.

gaseosa (ga-say-OH-sah)
Soft drink

junta
A small group ruling a country, especially after a coup and before a legal government has been elected.

ladino
Any person—whether of European, Indian, or mestizo descent—who speaks Spanish and is Westernized.

machismo
Latin American ideal of manliness.

matanza (mah-TAN-zah)
Massacre or slaughter

madrino (ma-DREE-no)
Godmother

mesones (may-SON-ays)
Single-story buildings, usually rundown, consisting of a connected series of small, individual dwellings, surrounding a common courtyard.

mestizo
A person of mixed European and Indian ancestry.

Nahua
Language of the Pipil Indians.

oligarchy
A small group of people exercising political control, usually for corrupt and selfish purposes.

padrino (pa-DREE-no)
Godfather

pupusa (poo-POO-sah)
A thick corn tortilla filled with beans, meat, or cheese; a special dish of El Salvador.

pupusería (poo-poo-say-REE-ah)
A restaurant or food stall where pupusa is sold.

tugurios (tu-GU-ryos)
Shantytowns

FURTHER INFORMATION

BOOKS

Deem, James M. *Top Ten Countries of Recent Immigrants.* El Salvador. Berkeley Heights, NJ: Myreportlinks.com (Enslow Publishers, Inc.), 2004.

Montgomery, Tommie Sue. *Revolution in El Salvador: From Civil Strife to Civil Peace.* Boulder, CO: Westview Press, 1995.

Nickles, Greg. Lands, Peoples, and Cultures. *El Salvador: The People and Culture.* New York: Crabtree Publishing Company, 1997.

Sander, Renfield. Major World Nations. *El Salvador.* New York: Chelsea House Publications, 1997.

Shields, Charles J. and James D. Henderson. Let's Discover Central America. *El Salvador.* Brookshire, TX: Mason Crest Publishers, 2002.

WEBSITES

Central Intelligence Agency World Factbook Webpage of El Salvador.
    www.cia.gov/cia/publications/factbook/geos/es.html

Country Reports on El Salvador.
    www.countryreports.org/history/frd/cs/svtoc.asp?countryid=73&countryName=El%20Salvador

El Salvador country studies. www.country-studies.com/el-salvador

El Salvador history. http://workmall.com/wfb2001/el_salvador/el_salvador_history_index.html

Infoplease on El Salvador. www.infoplease.com/ipa/A0107489.html

Frommer's on El Salvador. www.frommers.com/destinations/salvador/2853010001.html

Lonely Planet World Guide to El Salvador History.
    www.lonelyplanet.com/destinations/ central_america/el_salvador/history.htm

Nationmaster on El Salvador. www.nationmaster.com/country/es

VIDEOS/DVDS

Decision to Win: First Fruits. New York: Third World Newsreel, 1984.

Innocent Voices. Los Angeles: 20th Century Fox, 2004.

MUSIC

40 Anos, Pese A Quien Pese. Universal Latino, 2004.

Cara O Cruz: Music of El Salvador. Flying Fish Records, 1992.

El Salvador... Mi Tierra. Salvavision, 2004.

Parrandon en el Salvador. Sony International, 2000.

BIBLIOGRAPHY

Argueta, Manlio. *One Day of Life*. New York: Vintage International, 1983.

Bachelis, Faren Maree. *El Salvador*. Chicago: Children's Press, 1990.

Barry, Tom. *El Salvador: A Country Guide*. Albuquerque: The Inter-Hemispheric Education Resource Center, 1990.

Haverstock, Nathan A. *El Salvador in Pictures*. Minneapolis: Lerner Publications, 1987.

Keller, Nancy, Tom Broasnahan, and Rob Rachowiecki. *Central America*. Berkeley, CA: Lonely Planet Publications, 1992.

INDEX